Secrete Gluon

Copyright 2015 by Marisa Cole

www.linkedin.com/in/salvadorsdolly

A Note From the Artist

Seattle, July 23 2015

I first studied art in the end of the 1980s. I largely only studied traditional art. I lived in my mind as a child and subsequentially my work was steeped in fantasy, surrealism, dada, visionary, science fiction and lowbrow art.

I have held many exhibitions since graduation in 1992. I have actually had my work exhibited along side the work of H.R. Giger, Ernst Fuchs, Marion Peck and even Salvador Dali. But I am far from known as an artist.

Over the years I have painted over 150 paintings. During the decades I also kept sketch books which I only rarely drew from life. I alwasy drew with a pen and therefore could not erase or modify the work. Some of these became paintings and were a successful. It is these I place in this book having family express a liking for the line doodles-drawings and the idea to colour them.

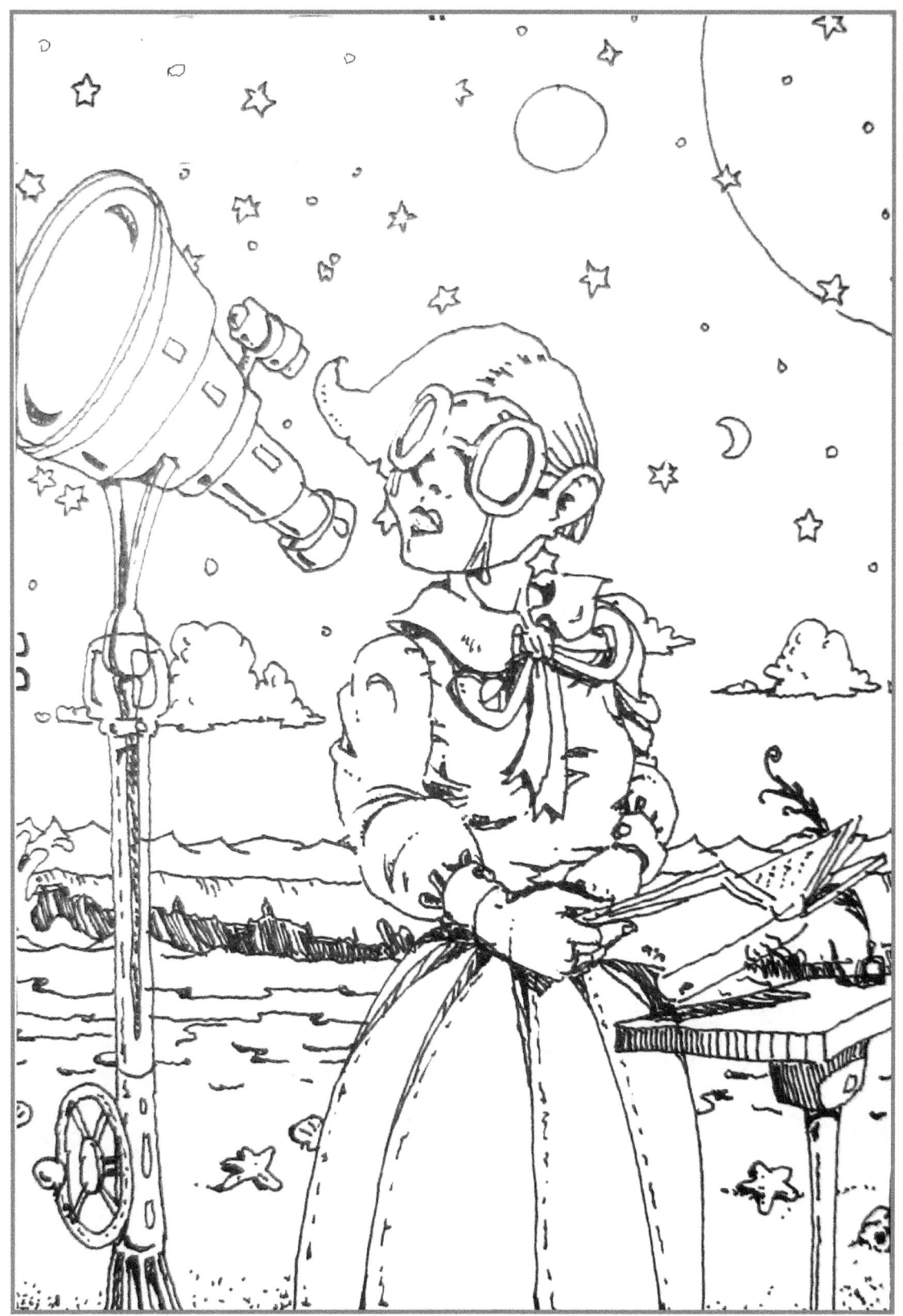

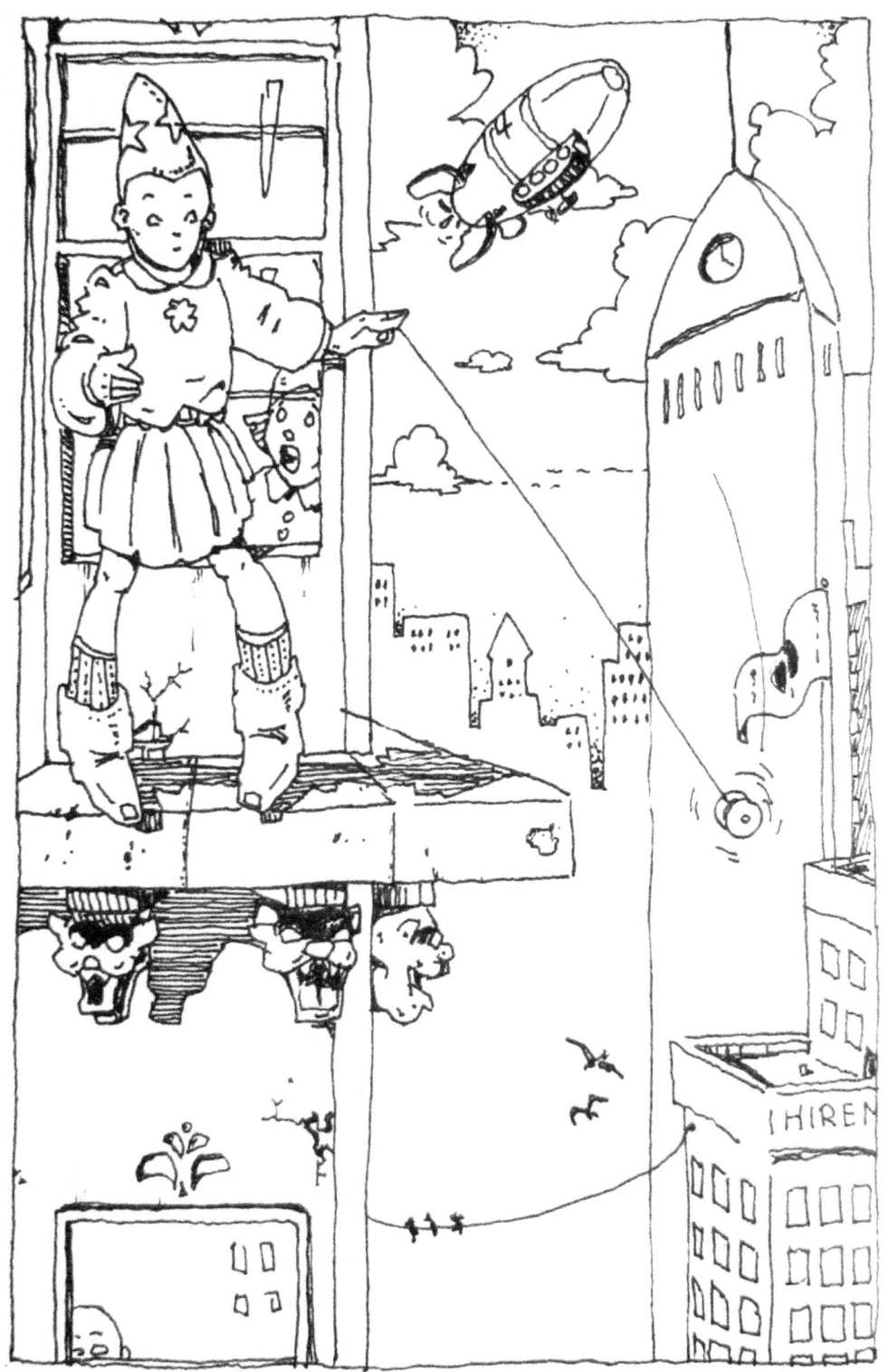

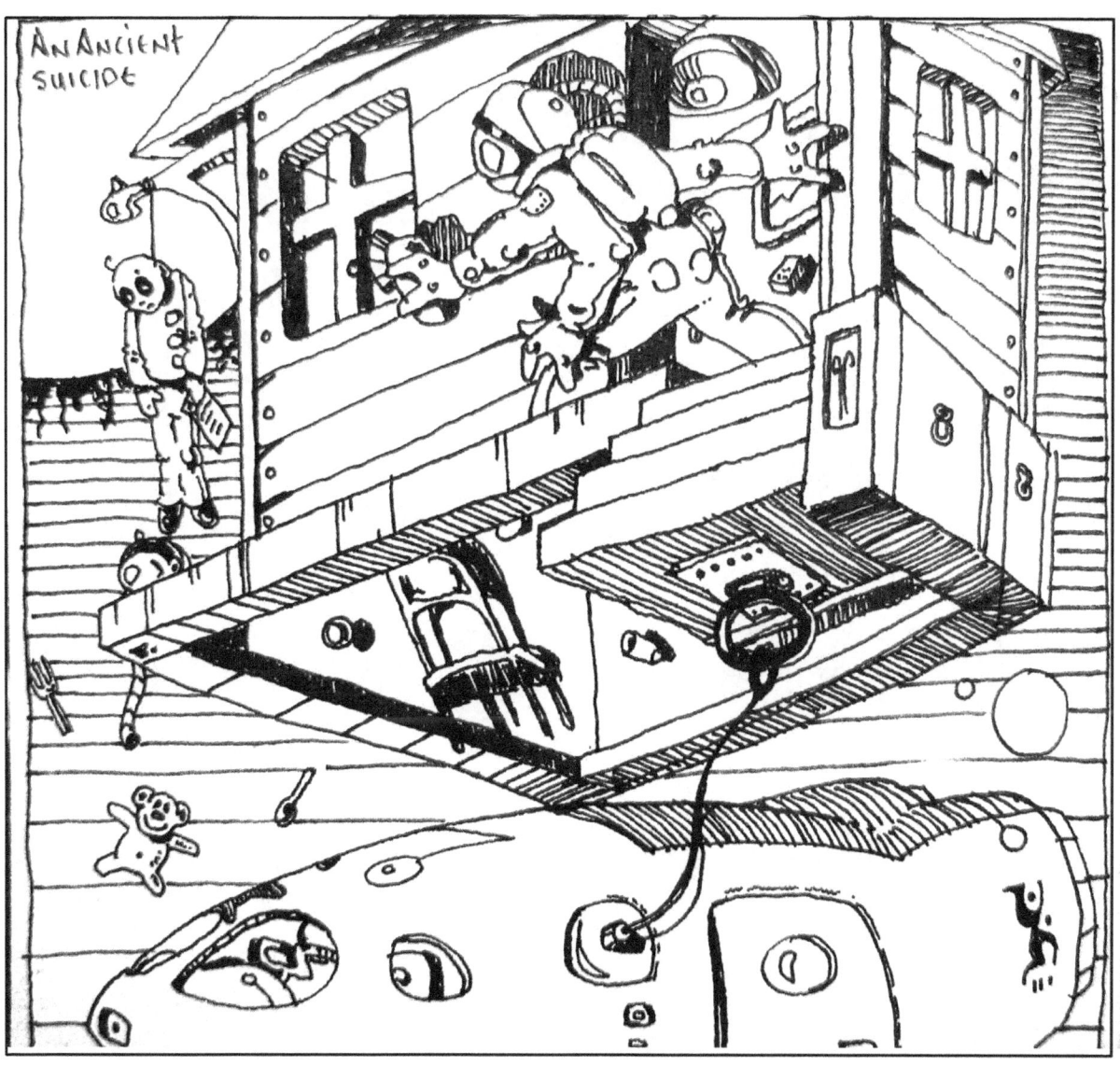

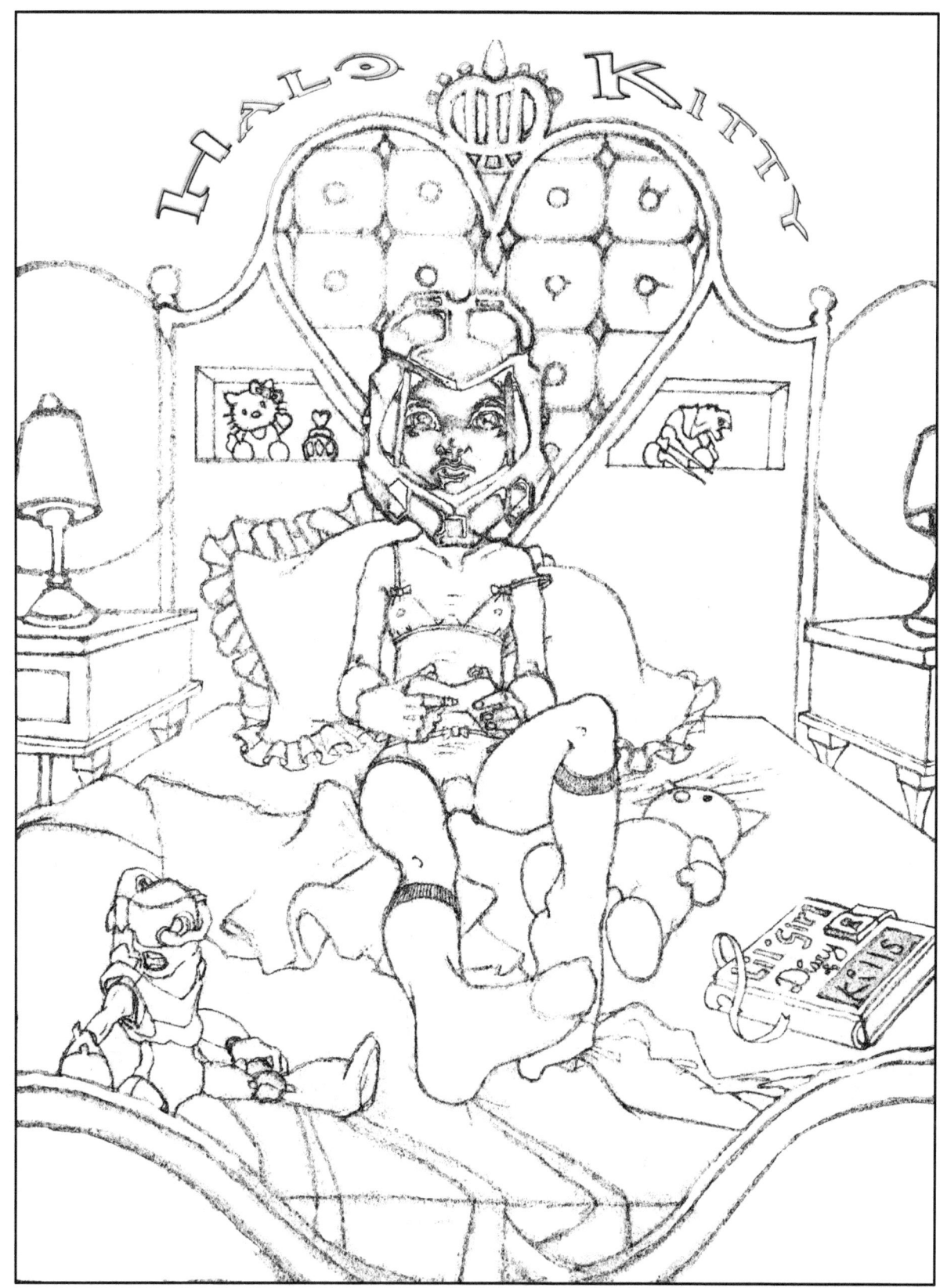

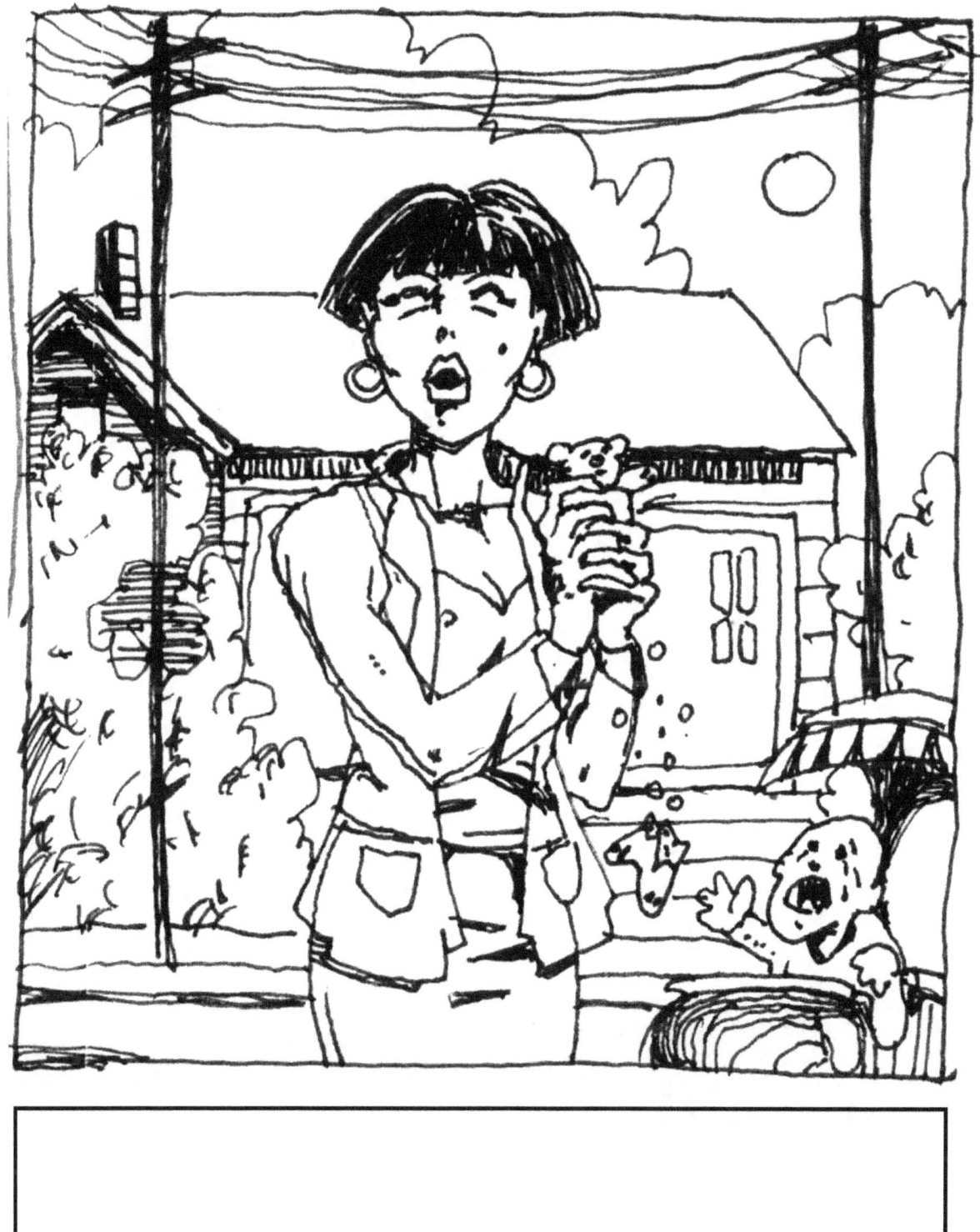

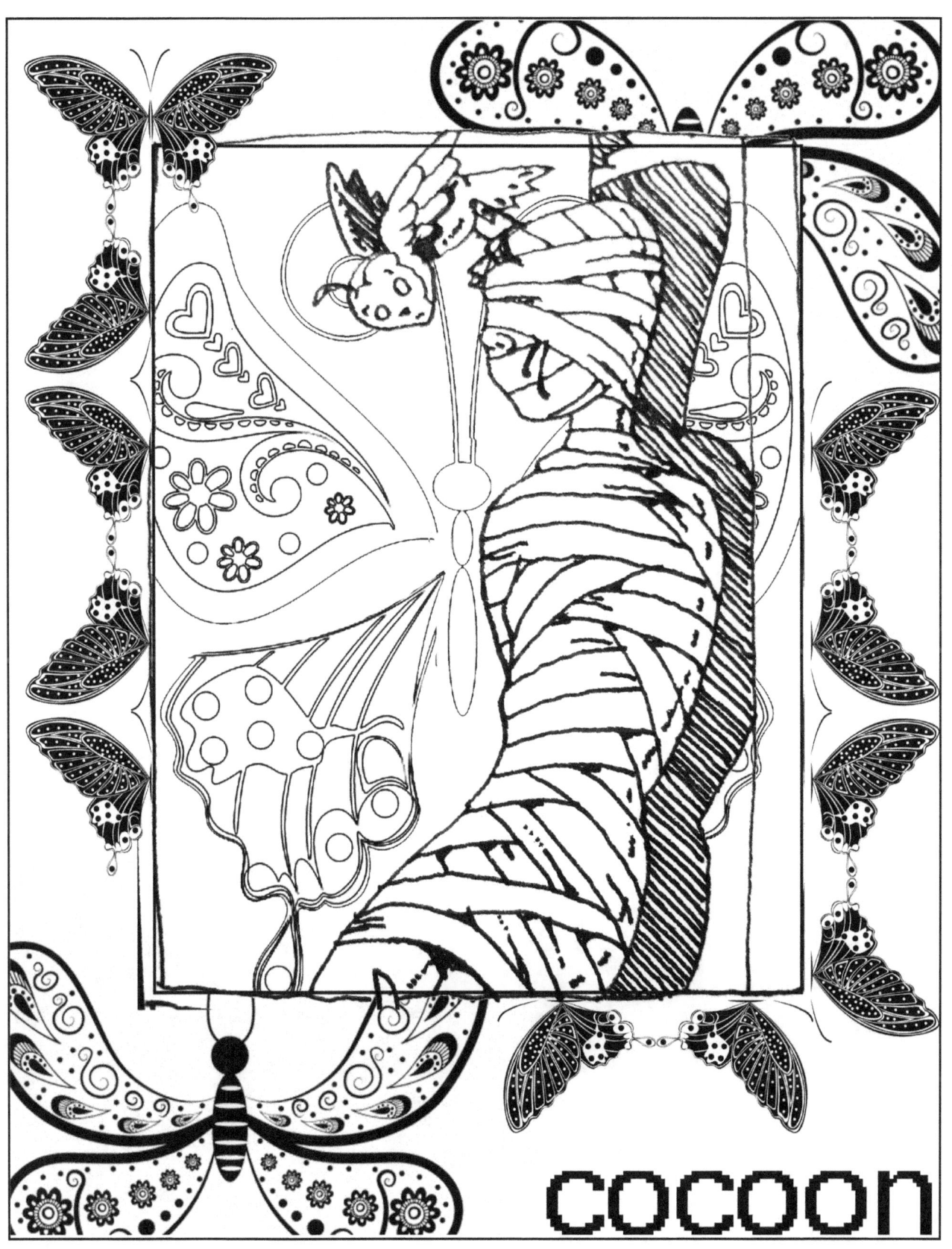

COCOON

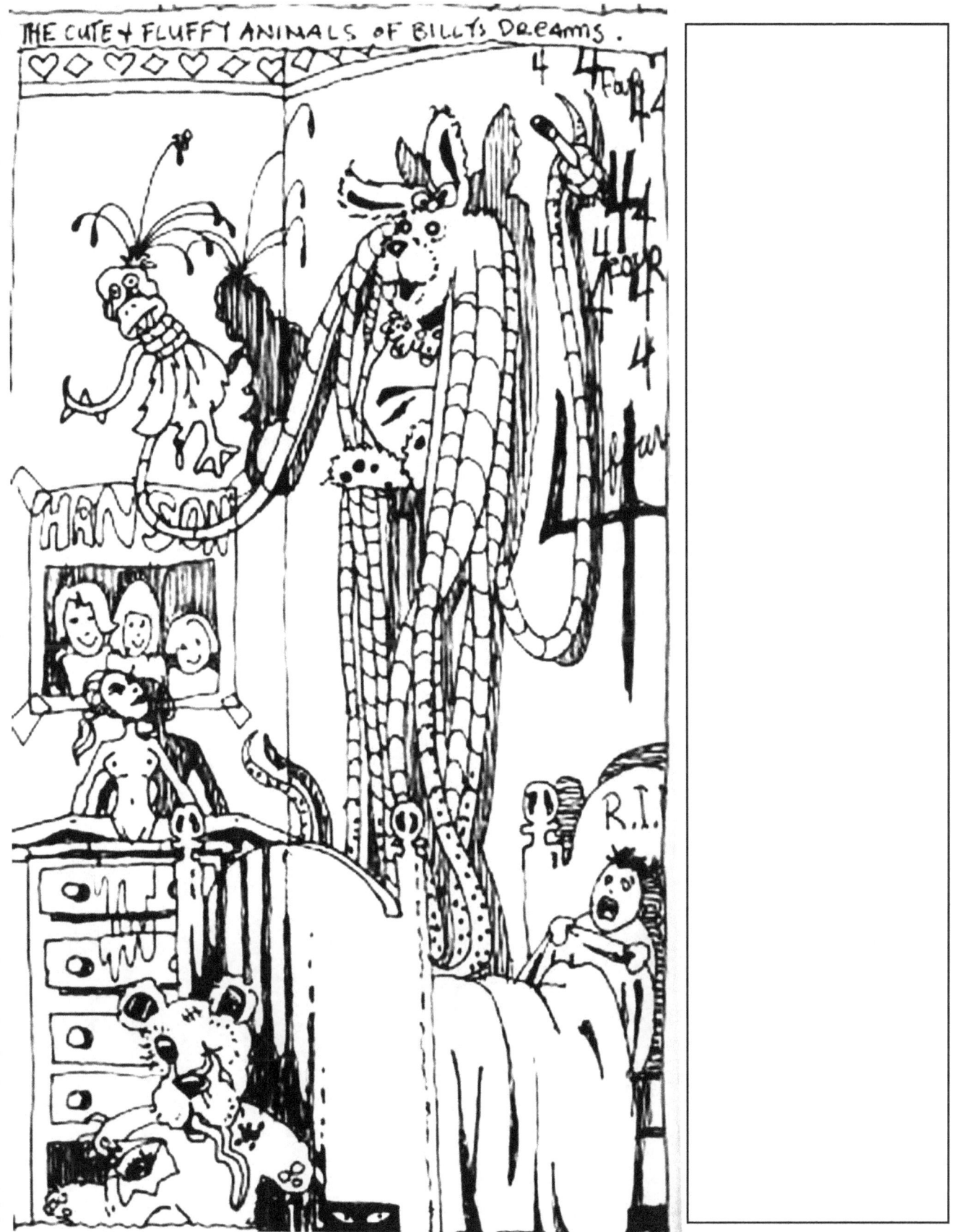

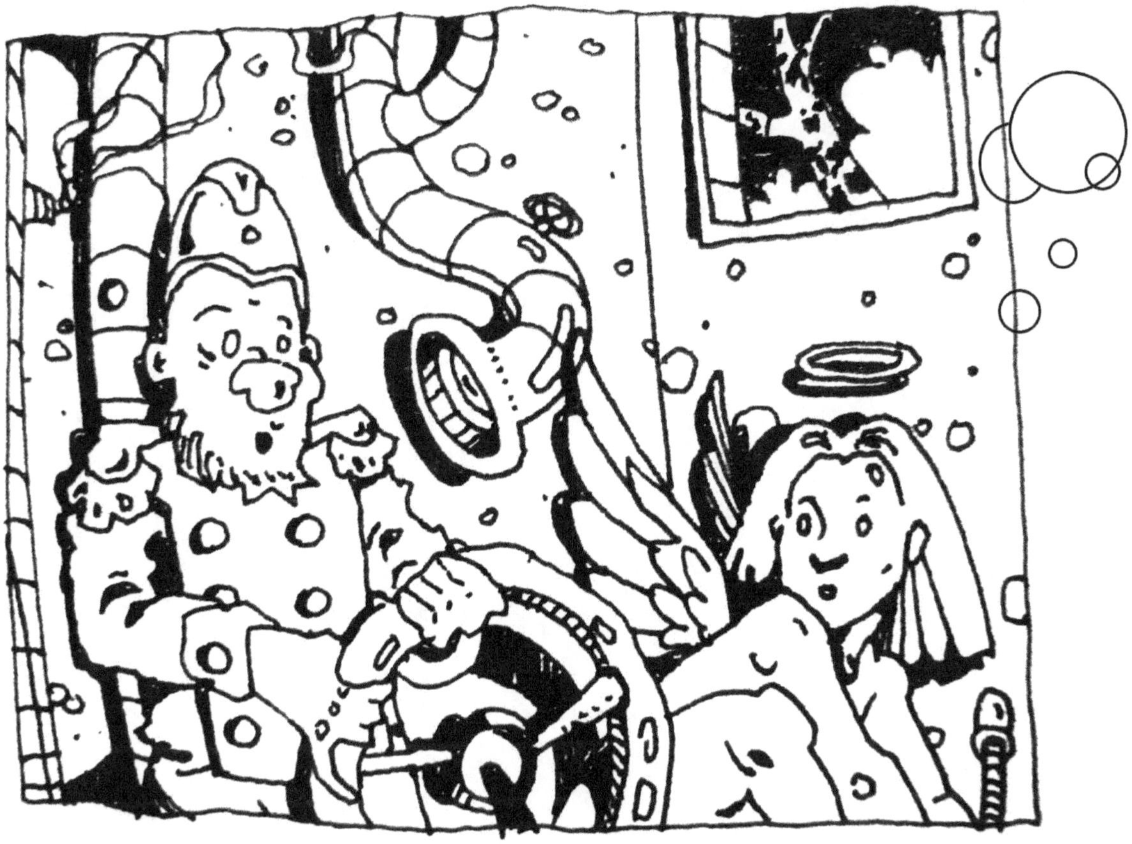

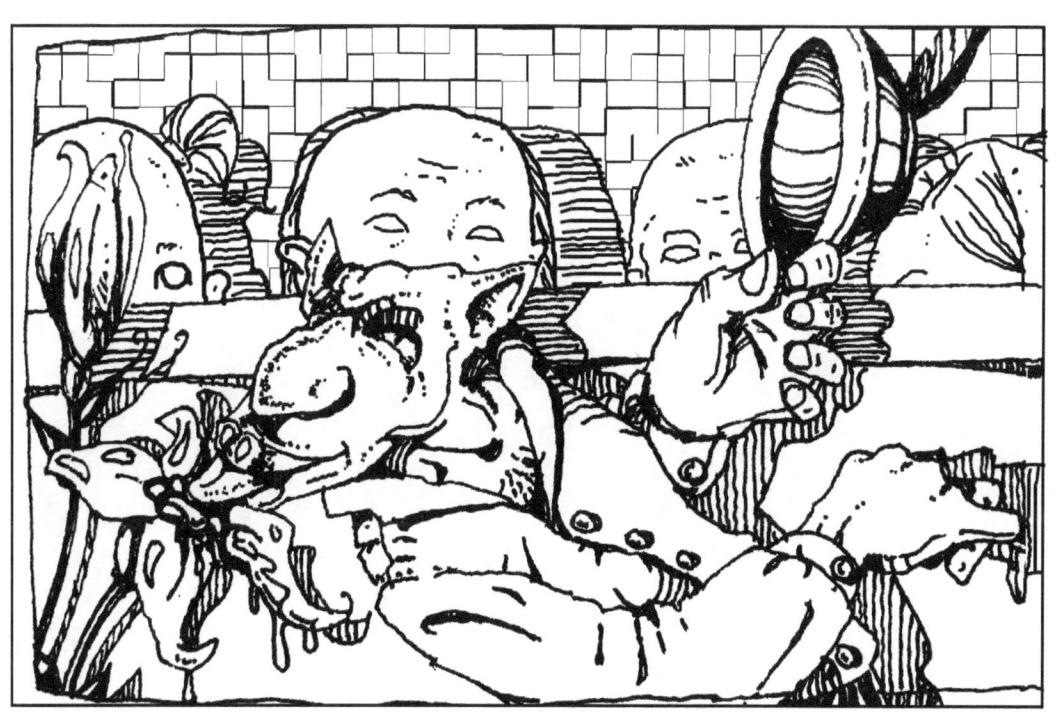

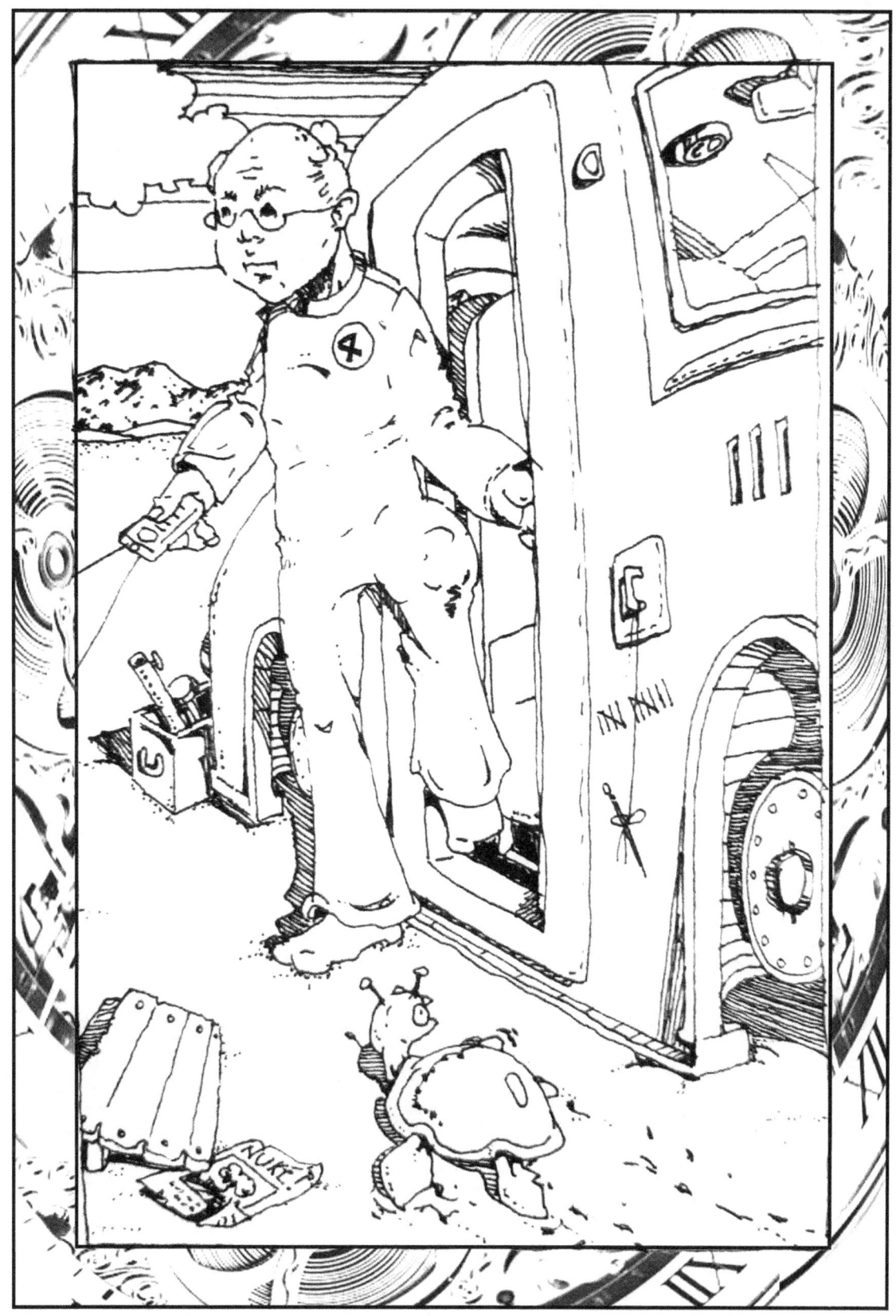

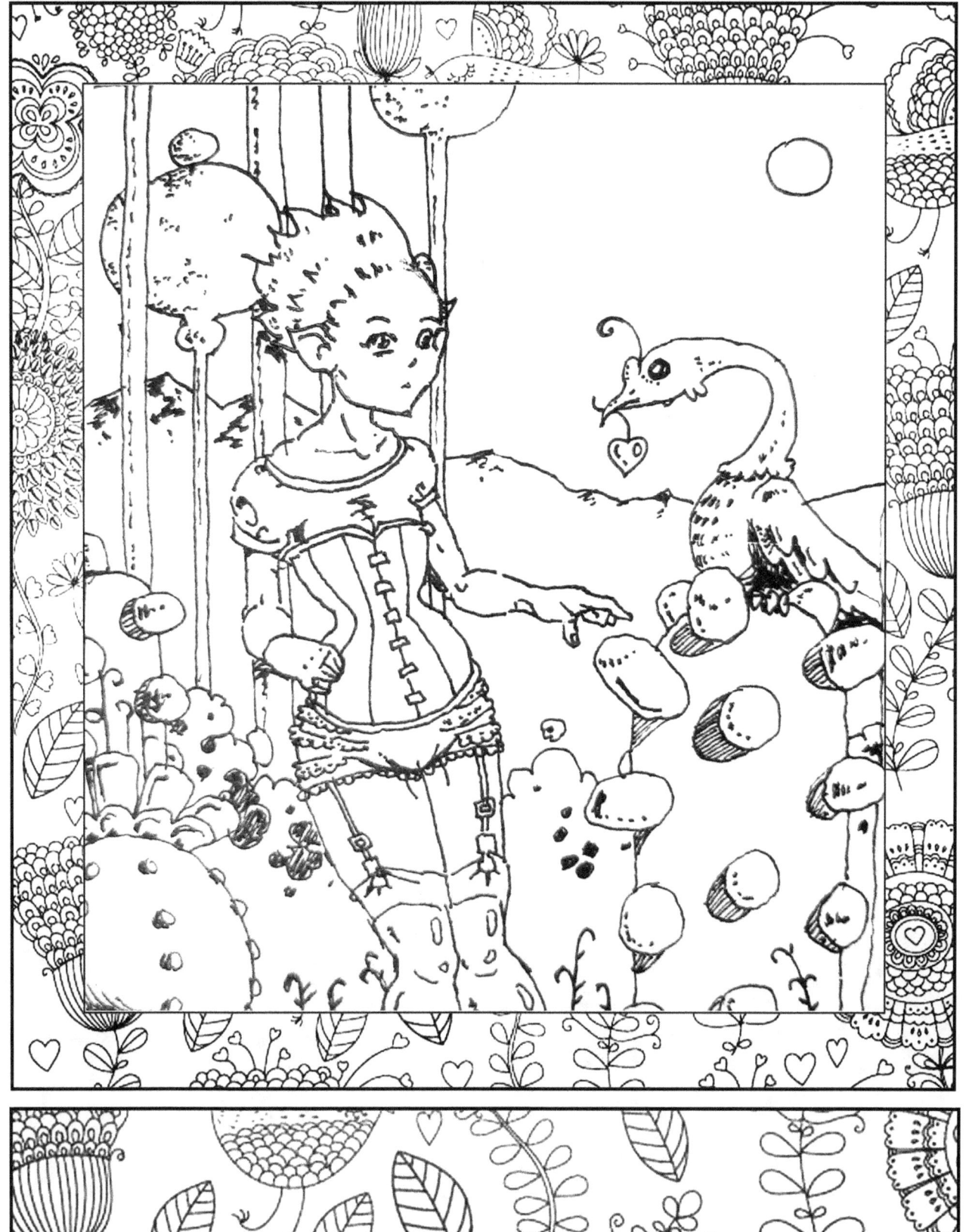

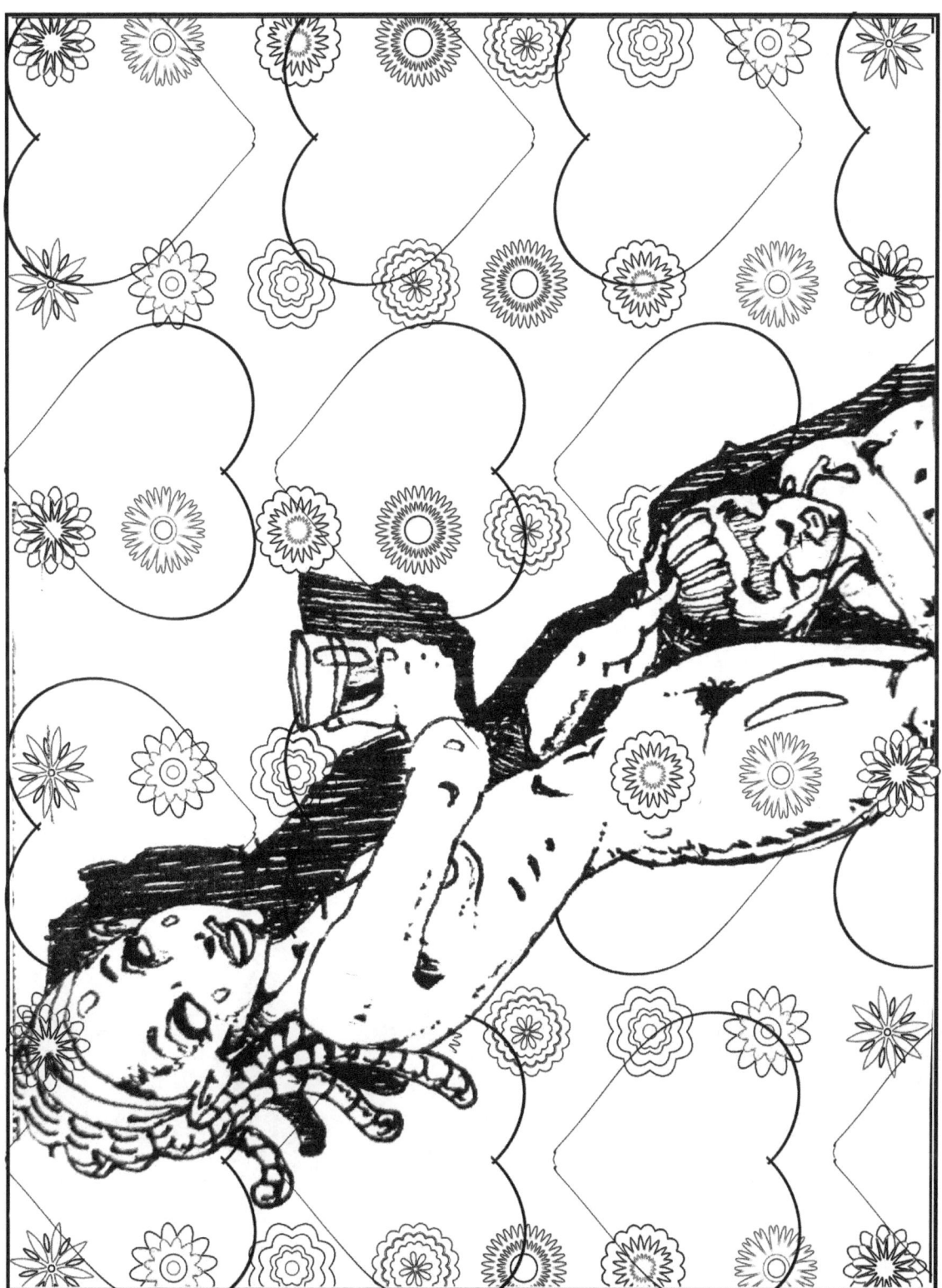

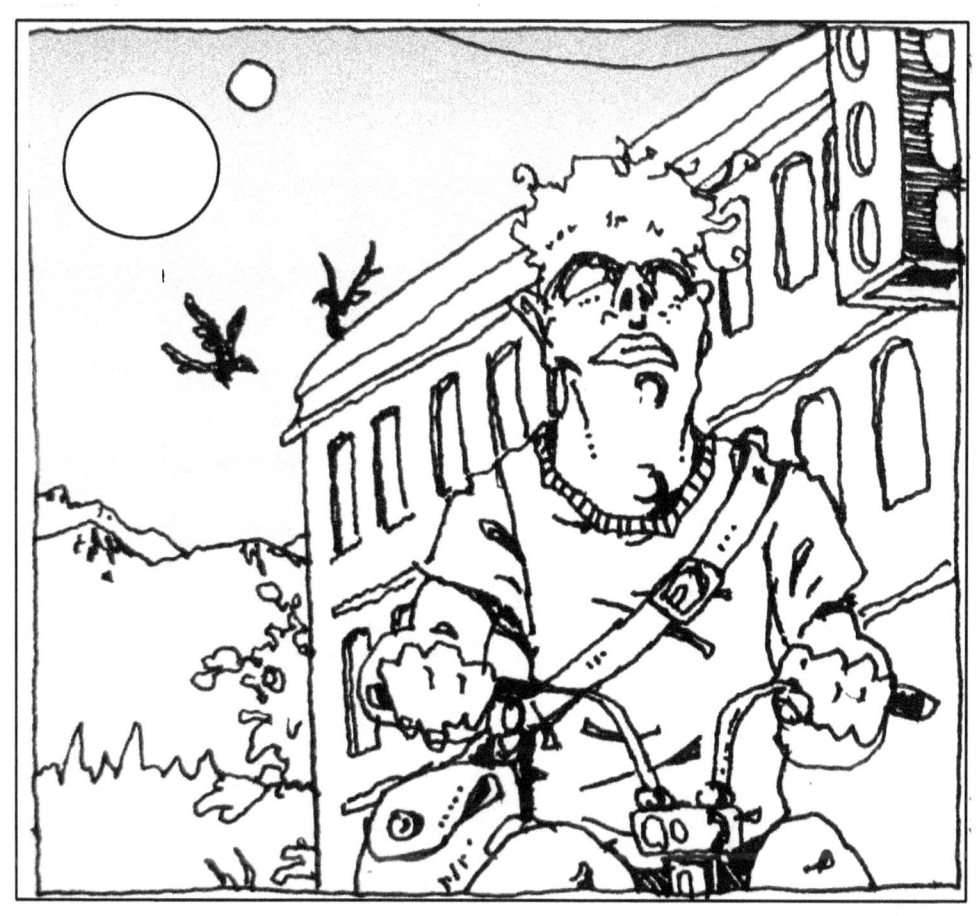

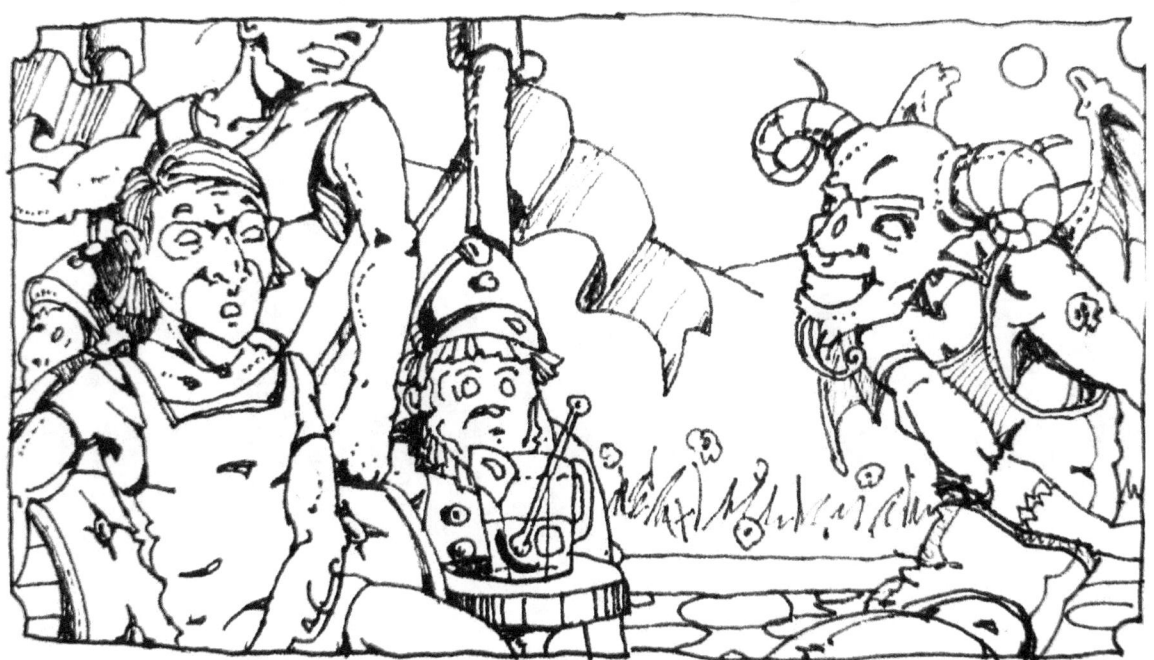

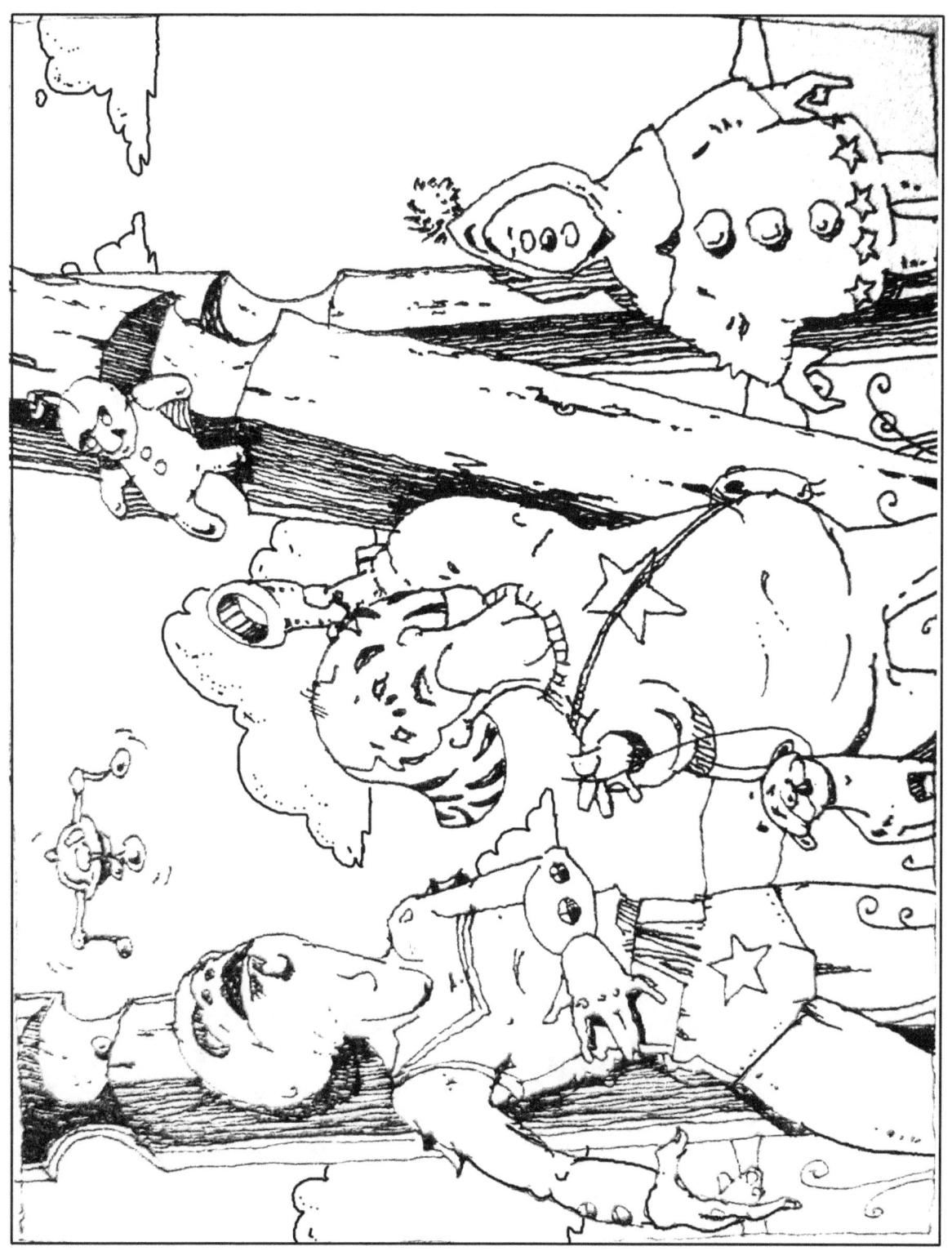

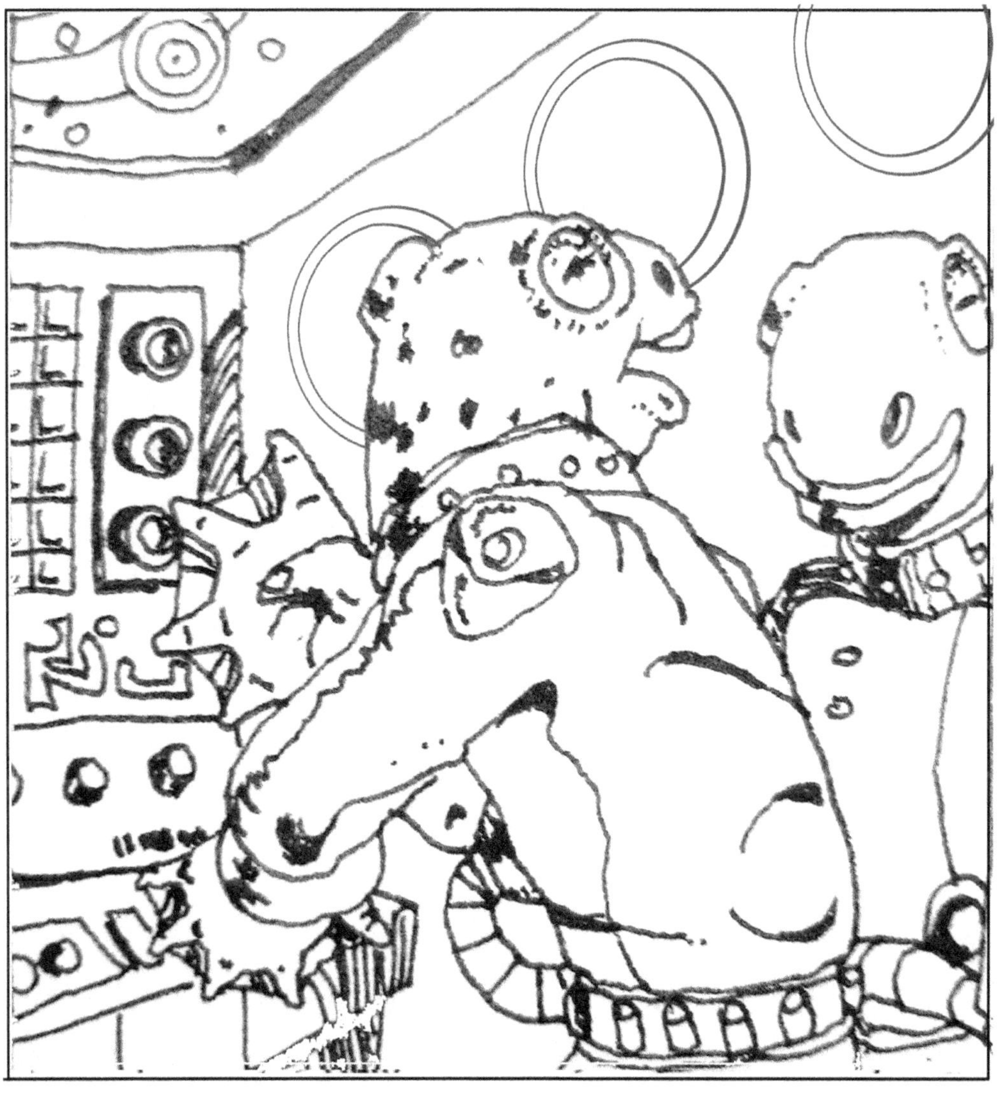

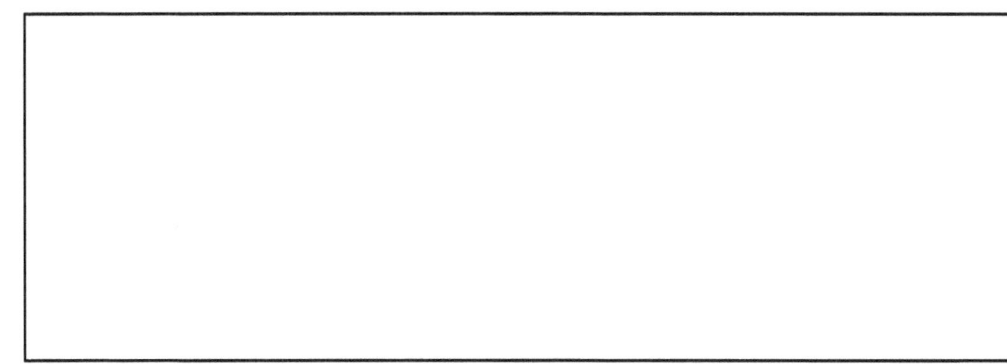

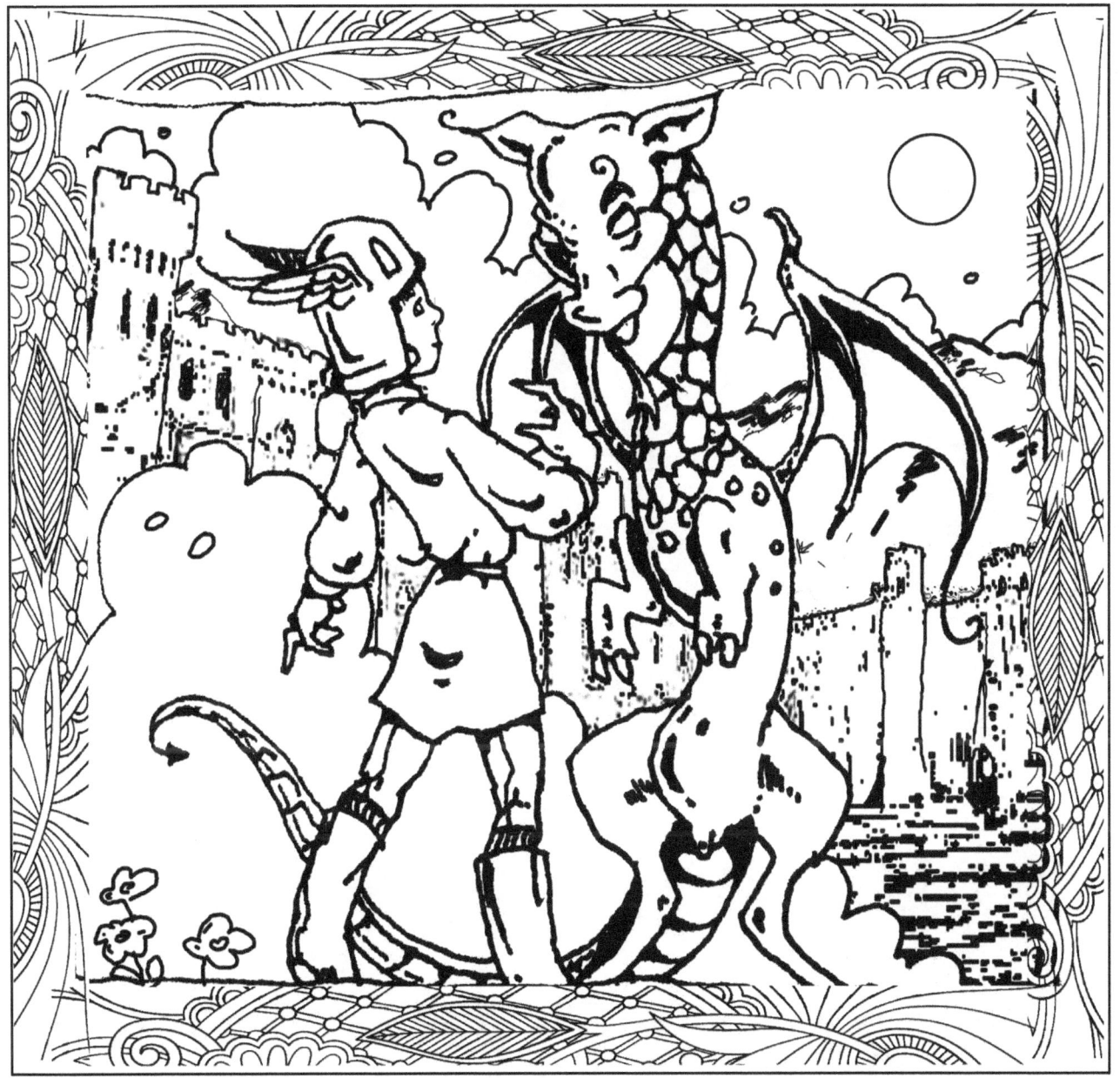

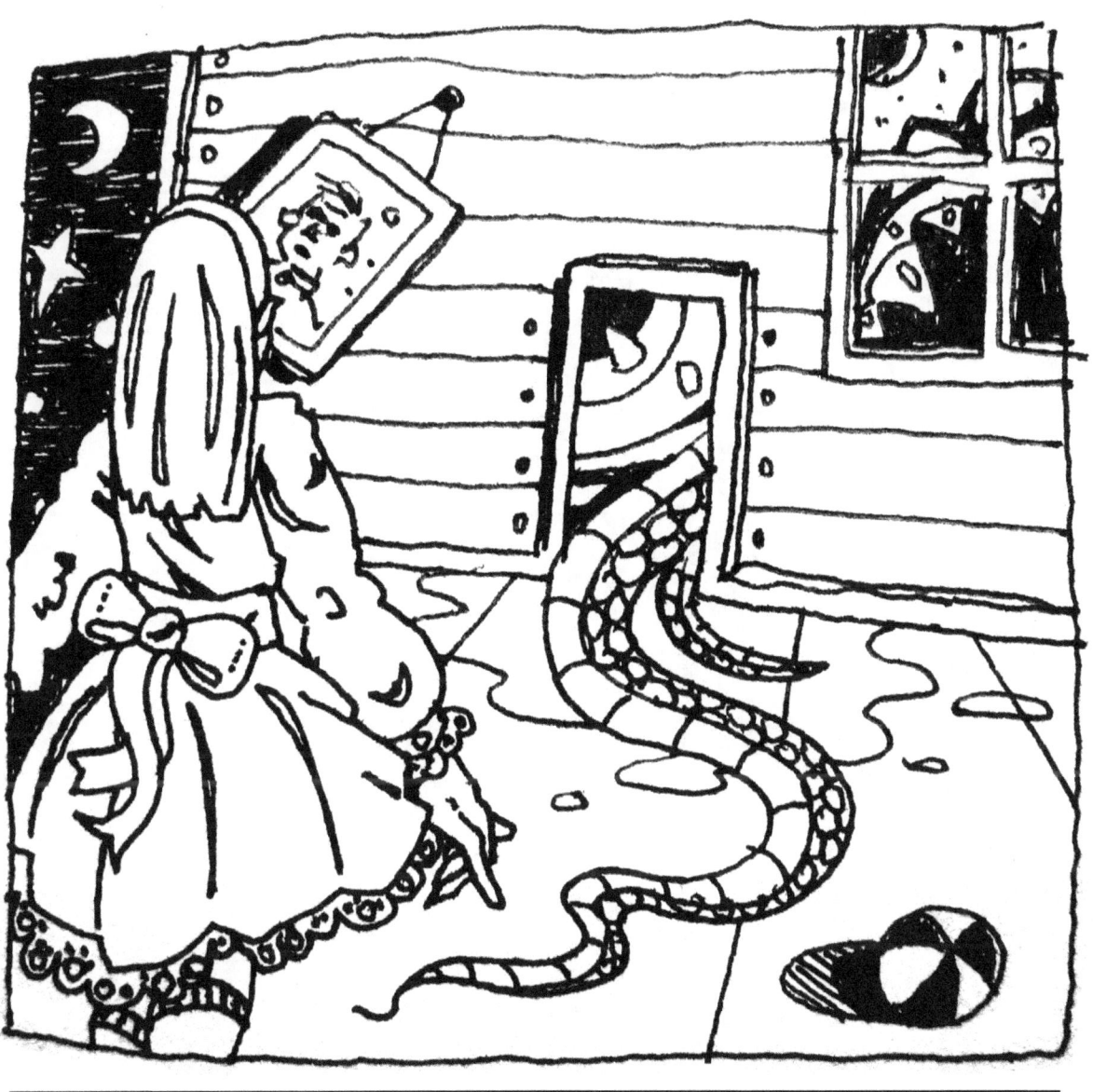

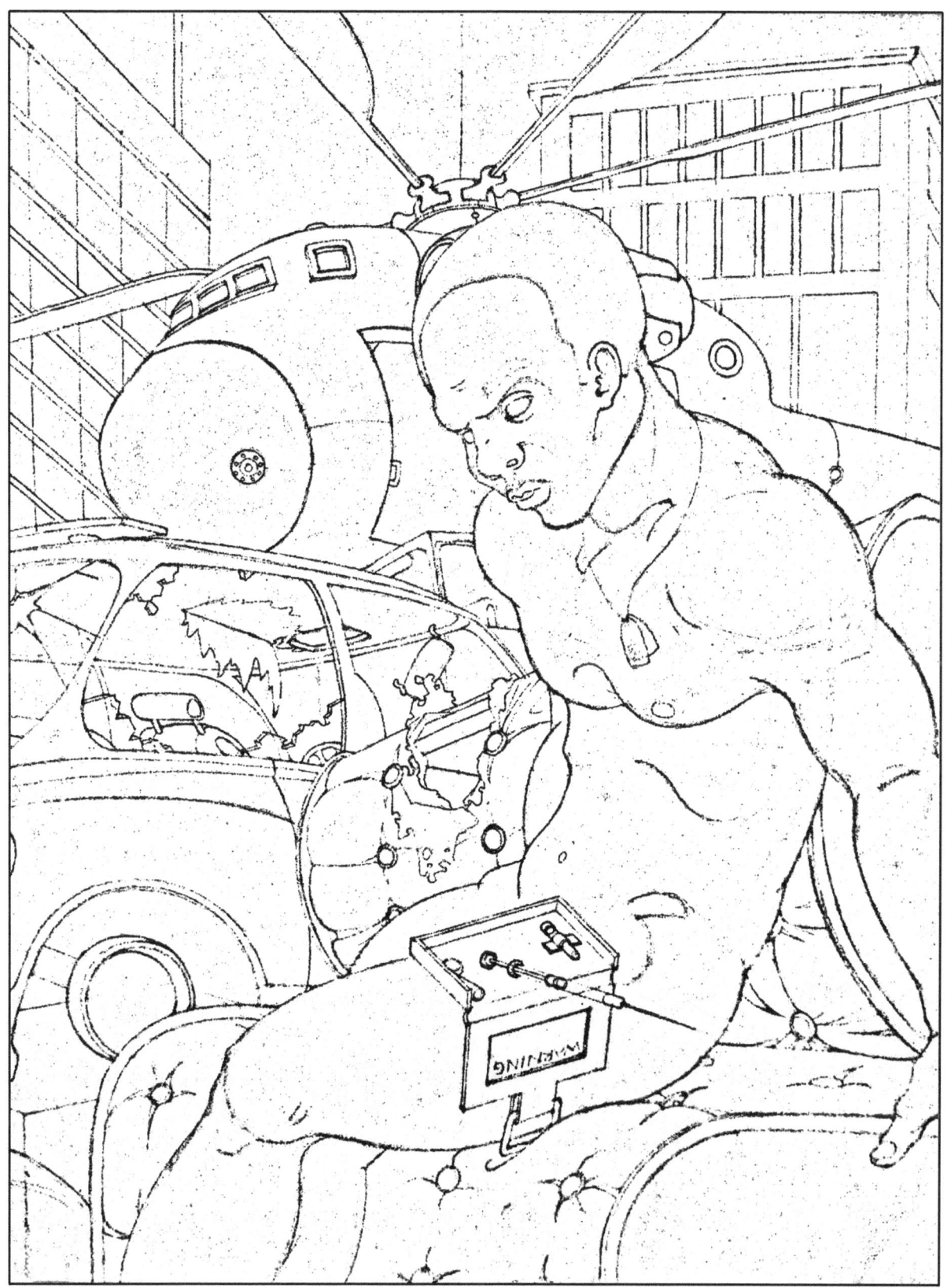

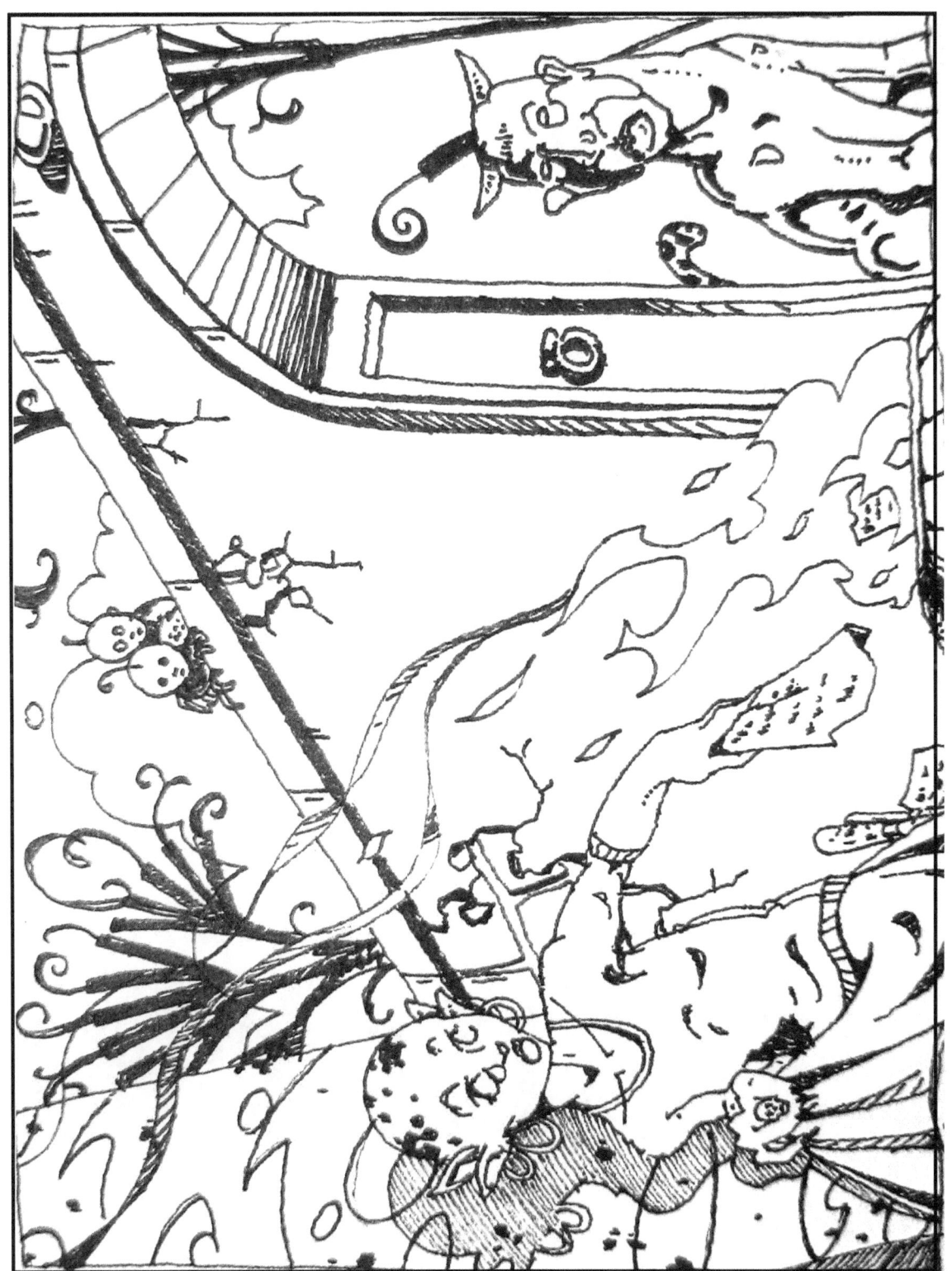

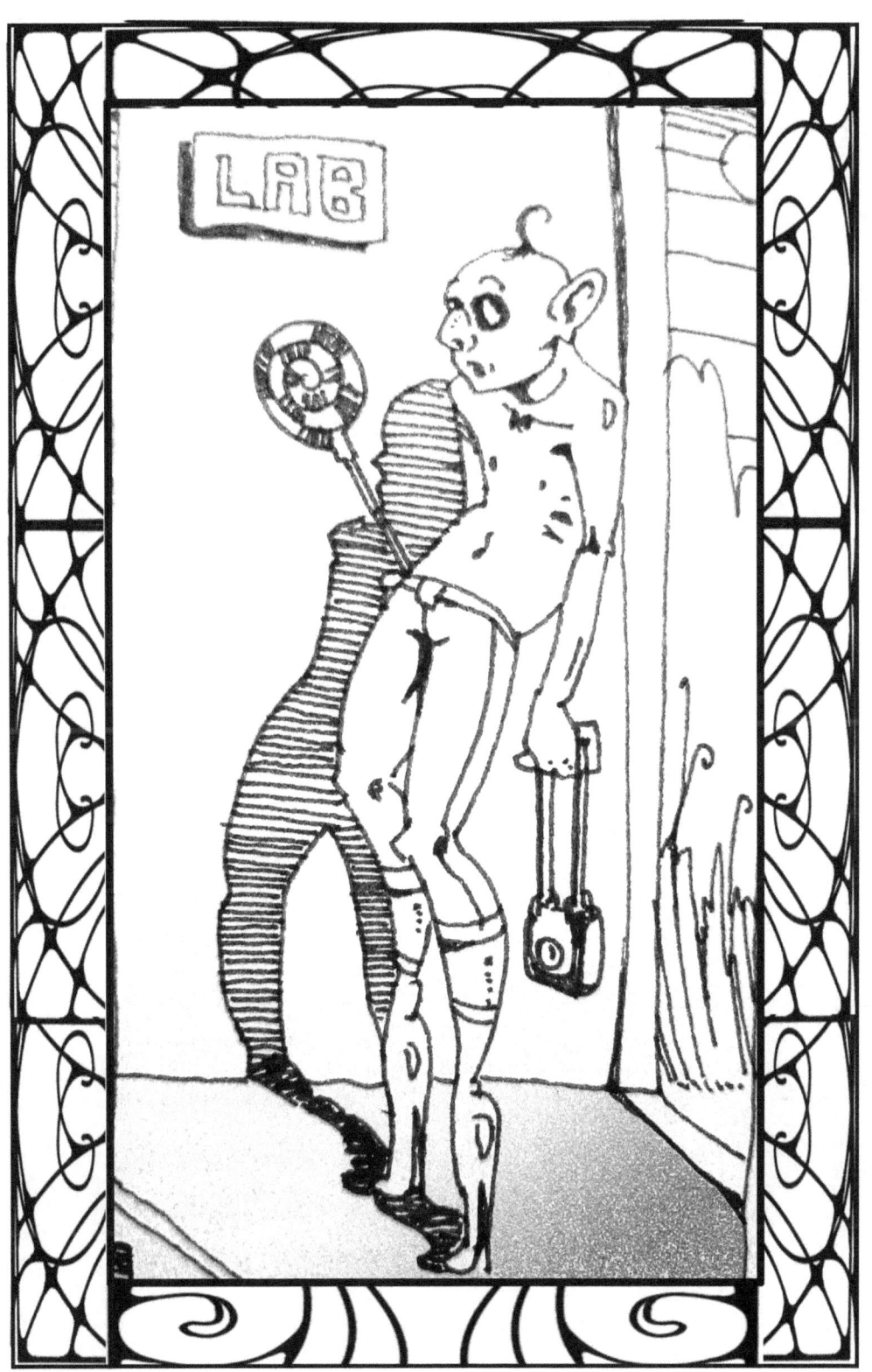

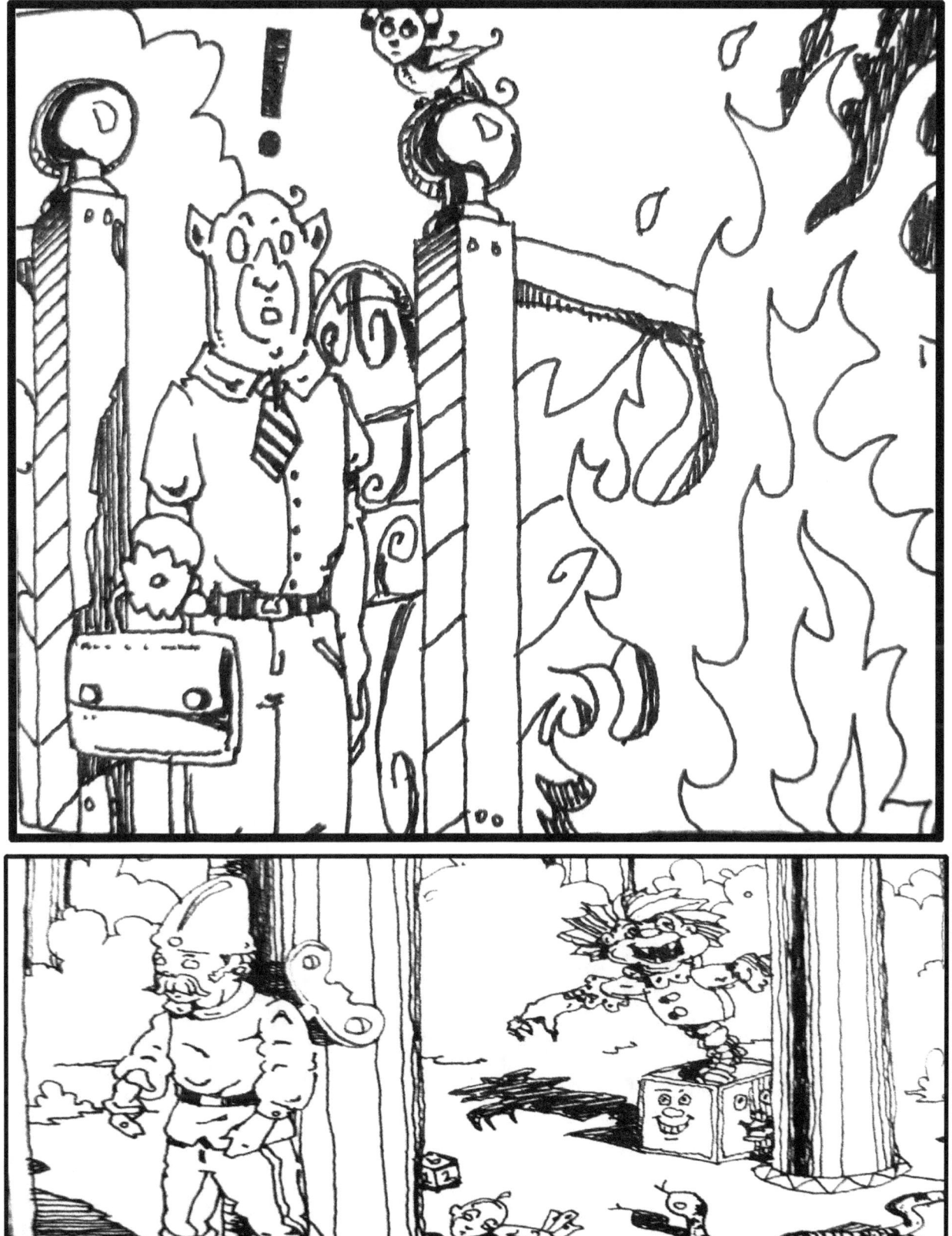

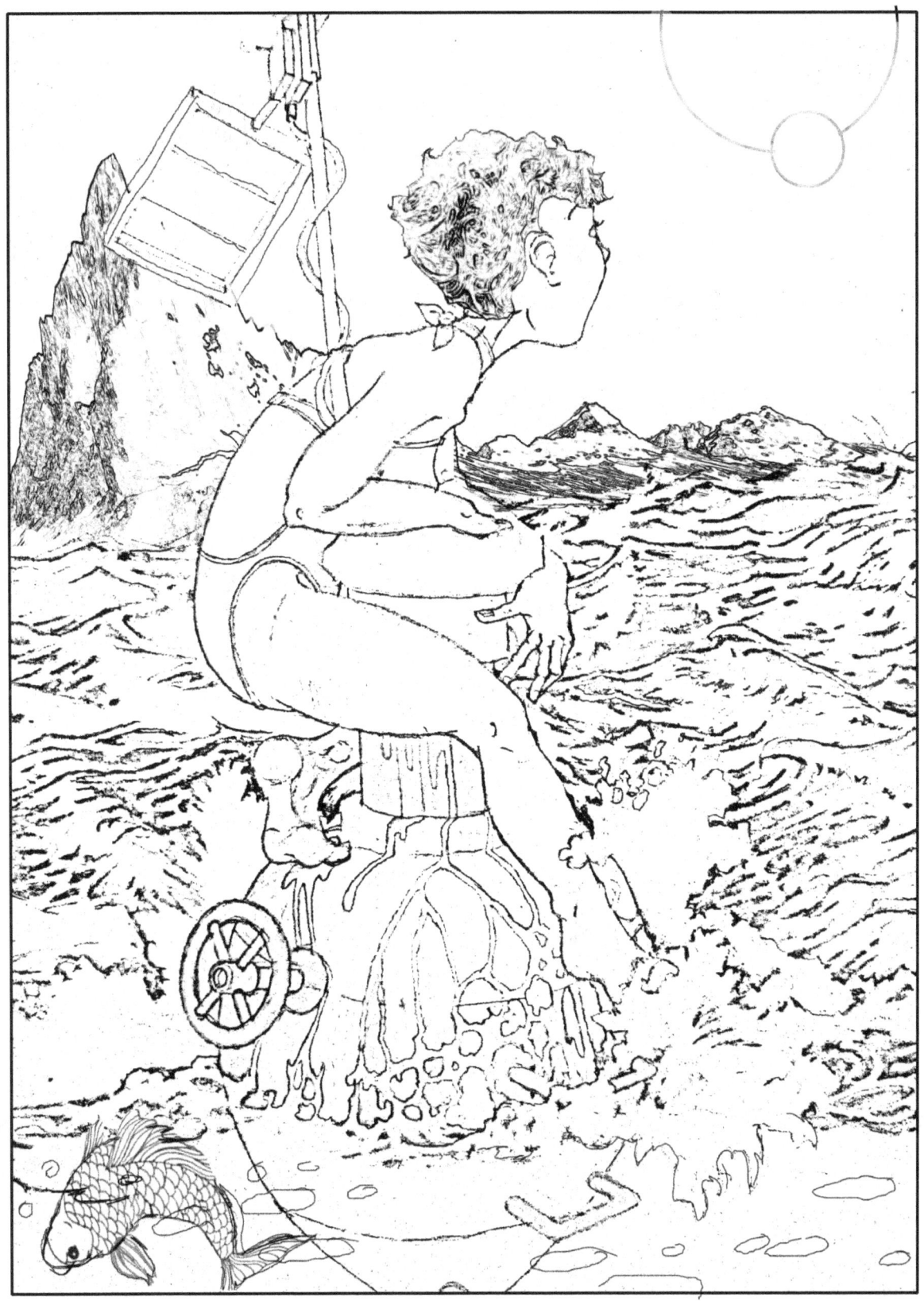

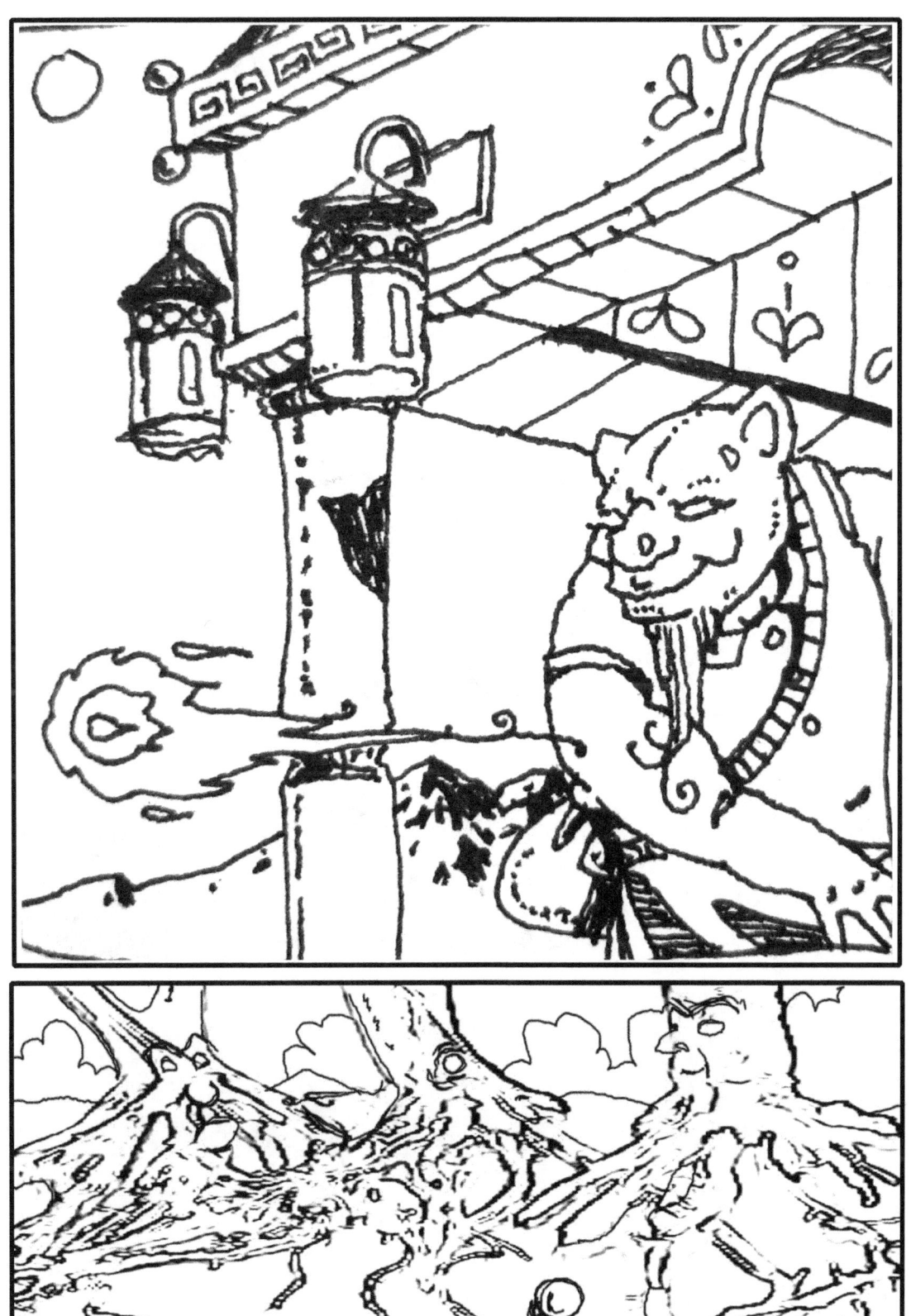

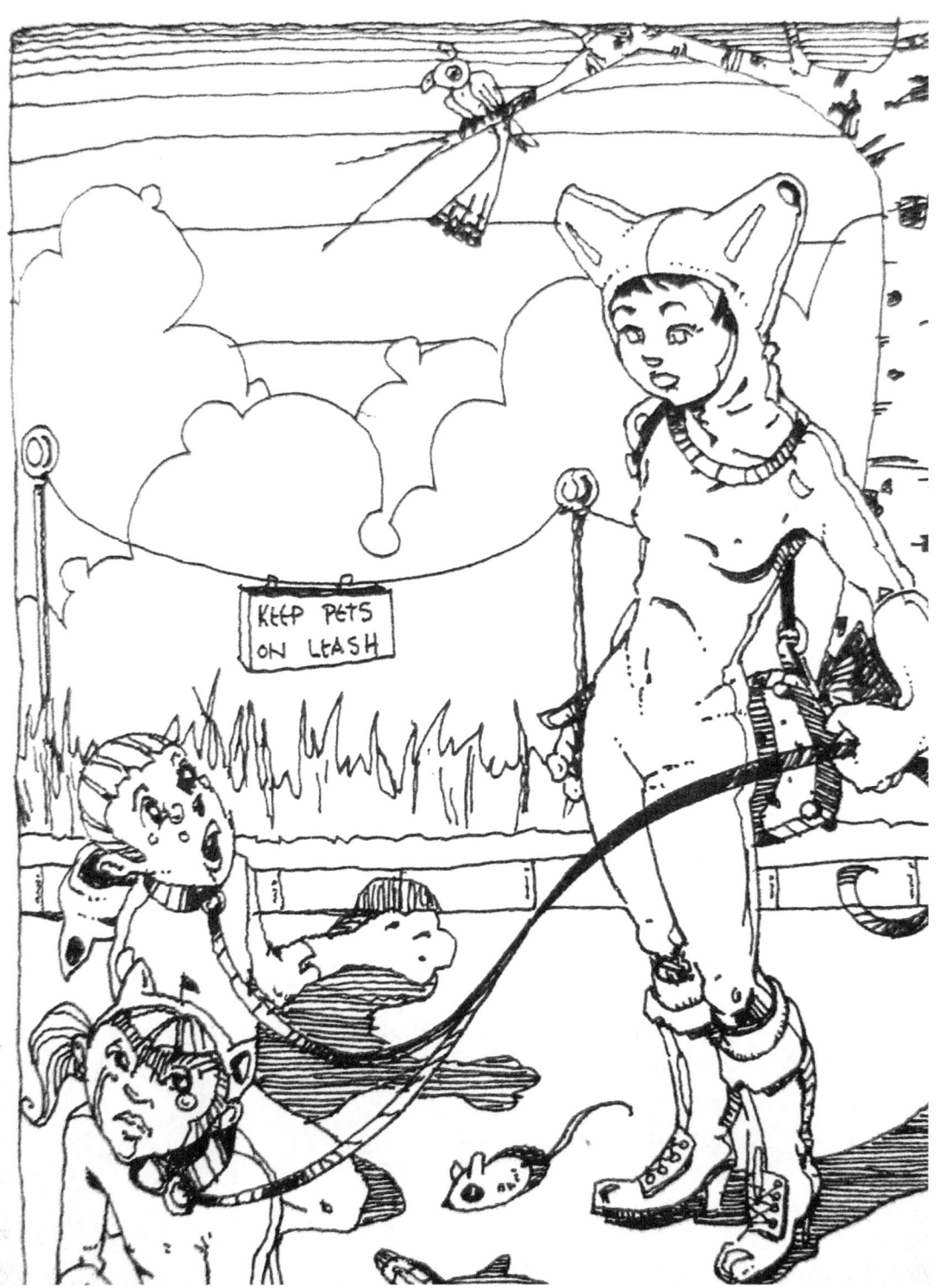

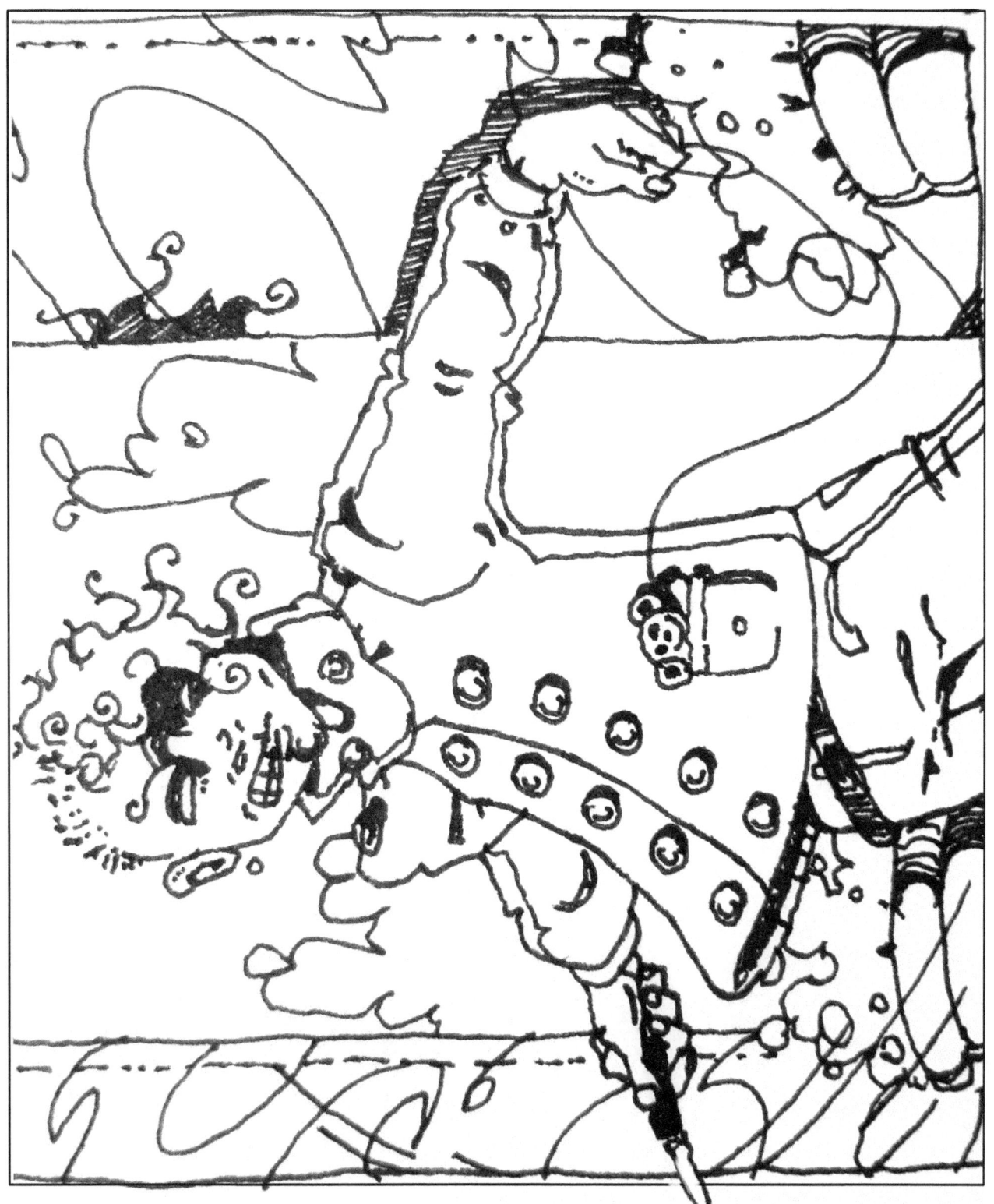

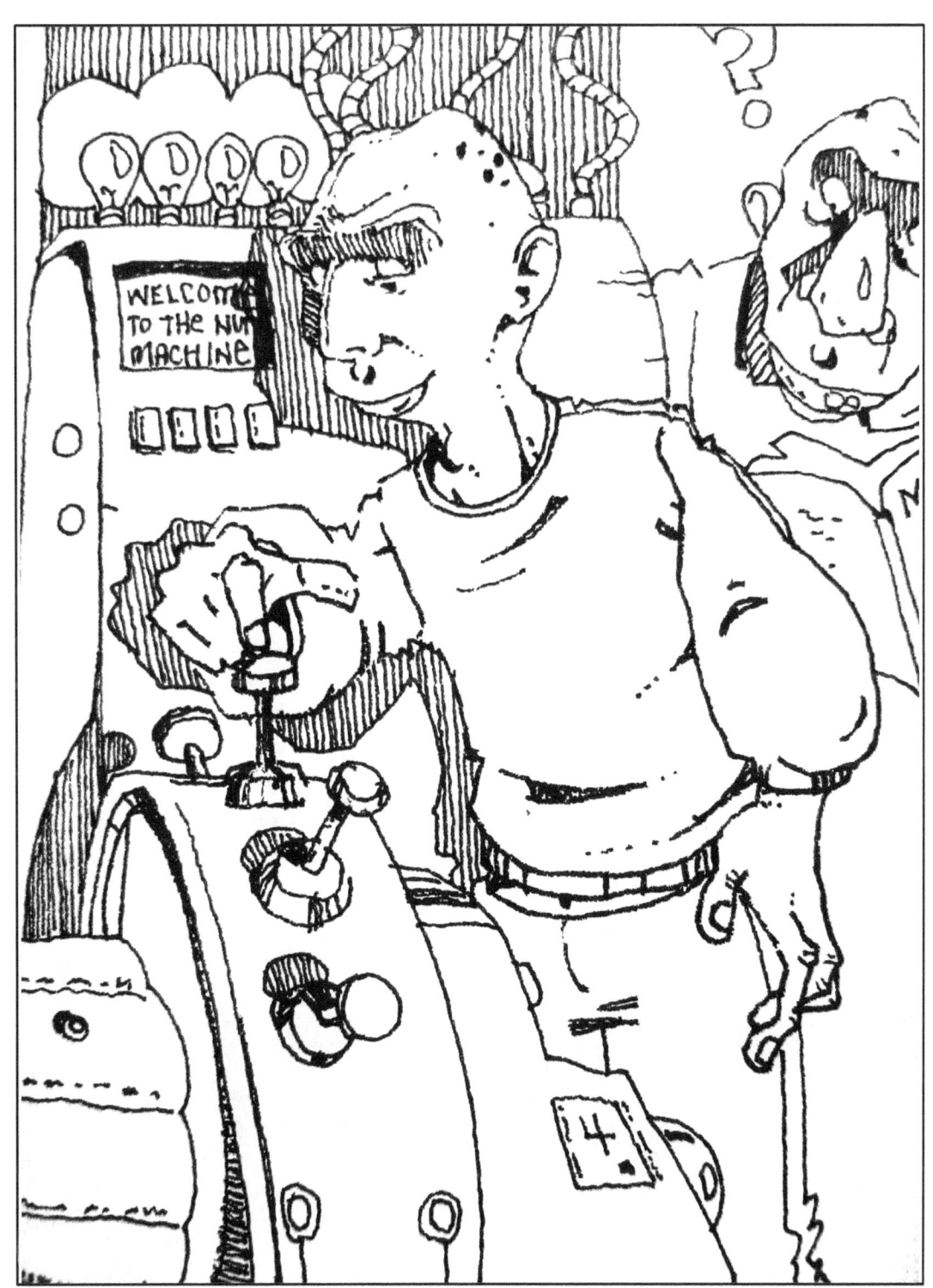

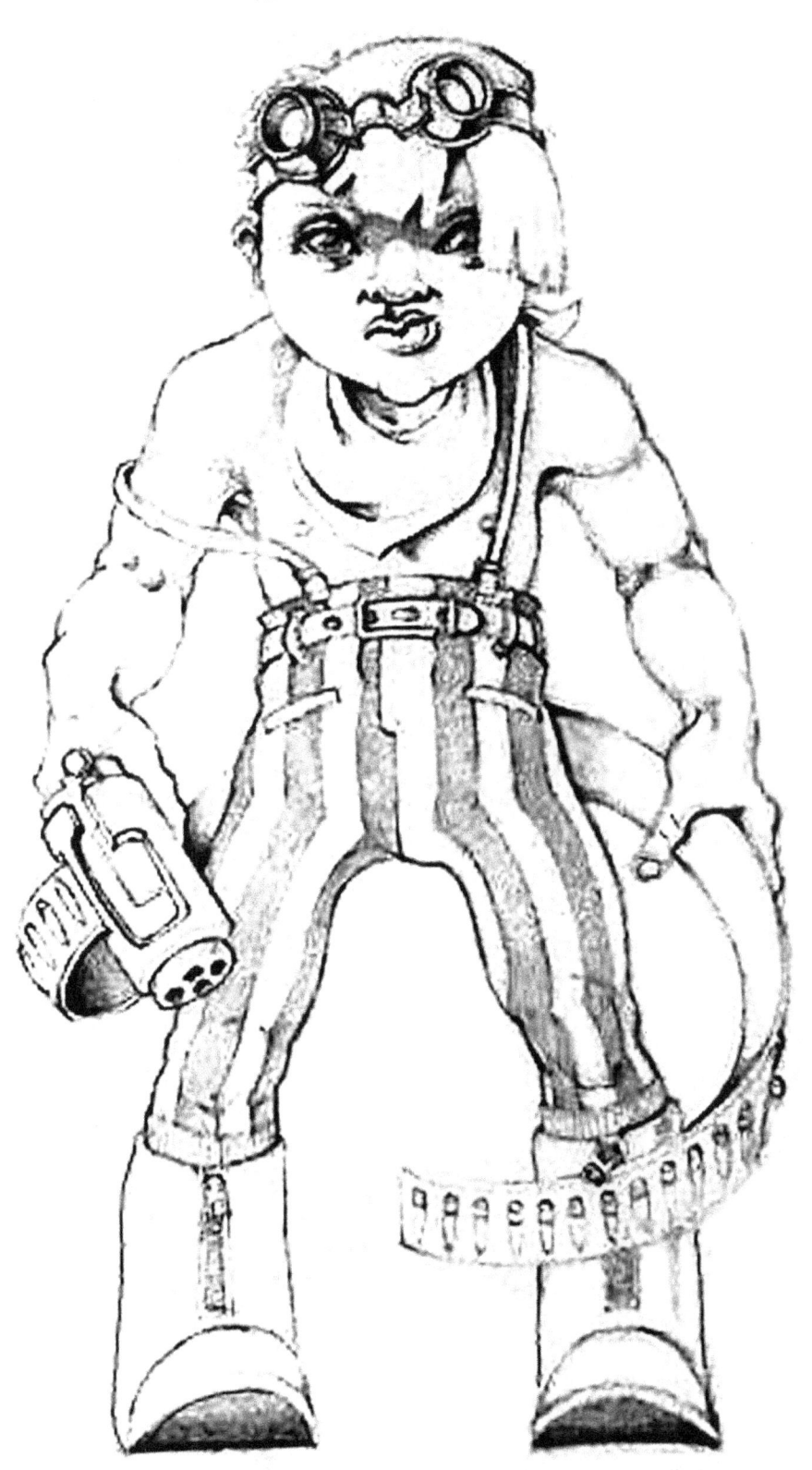

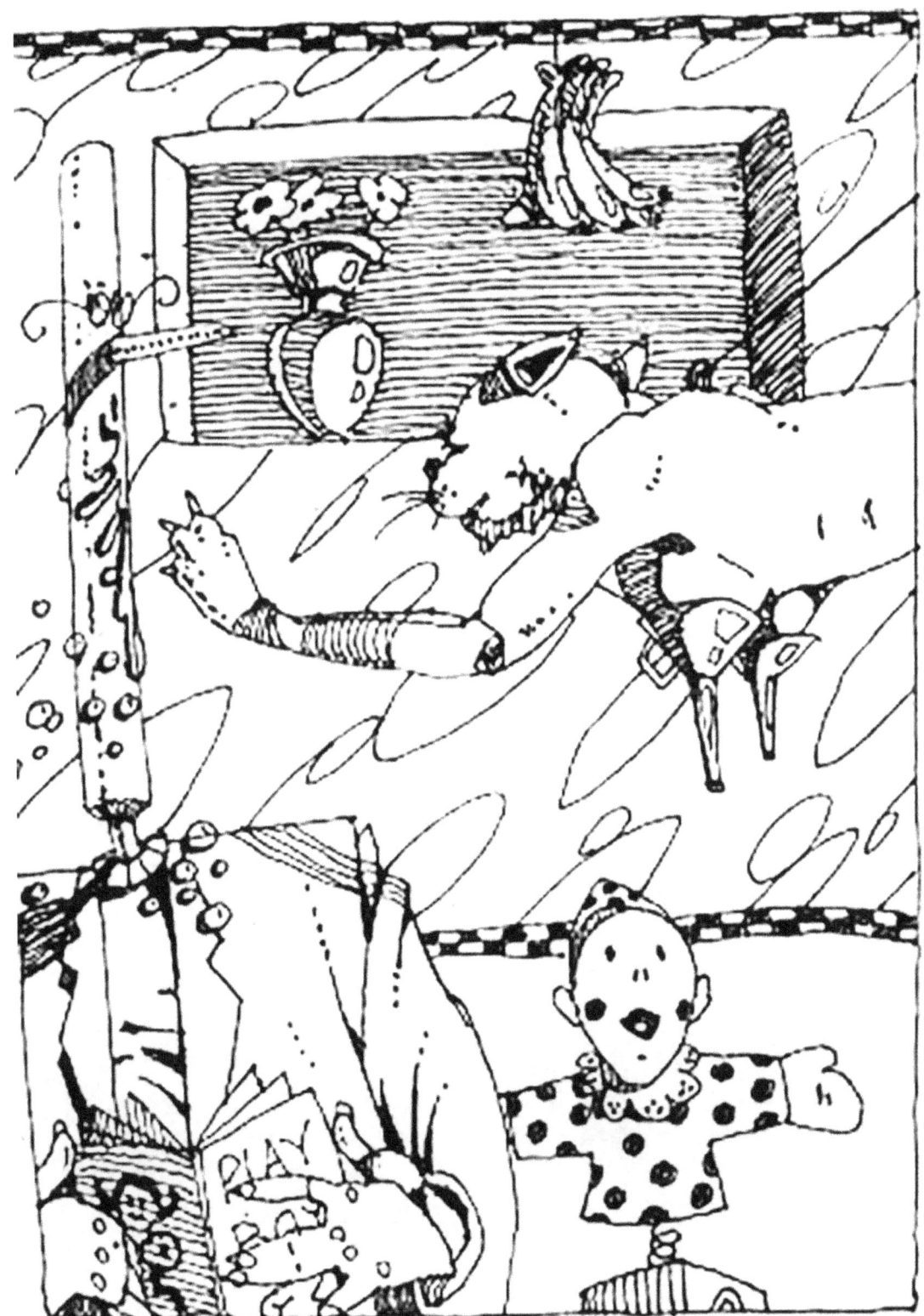

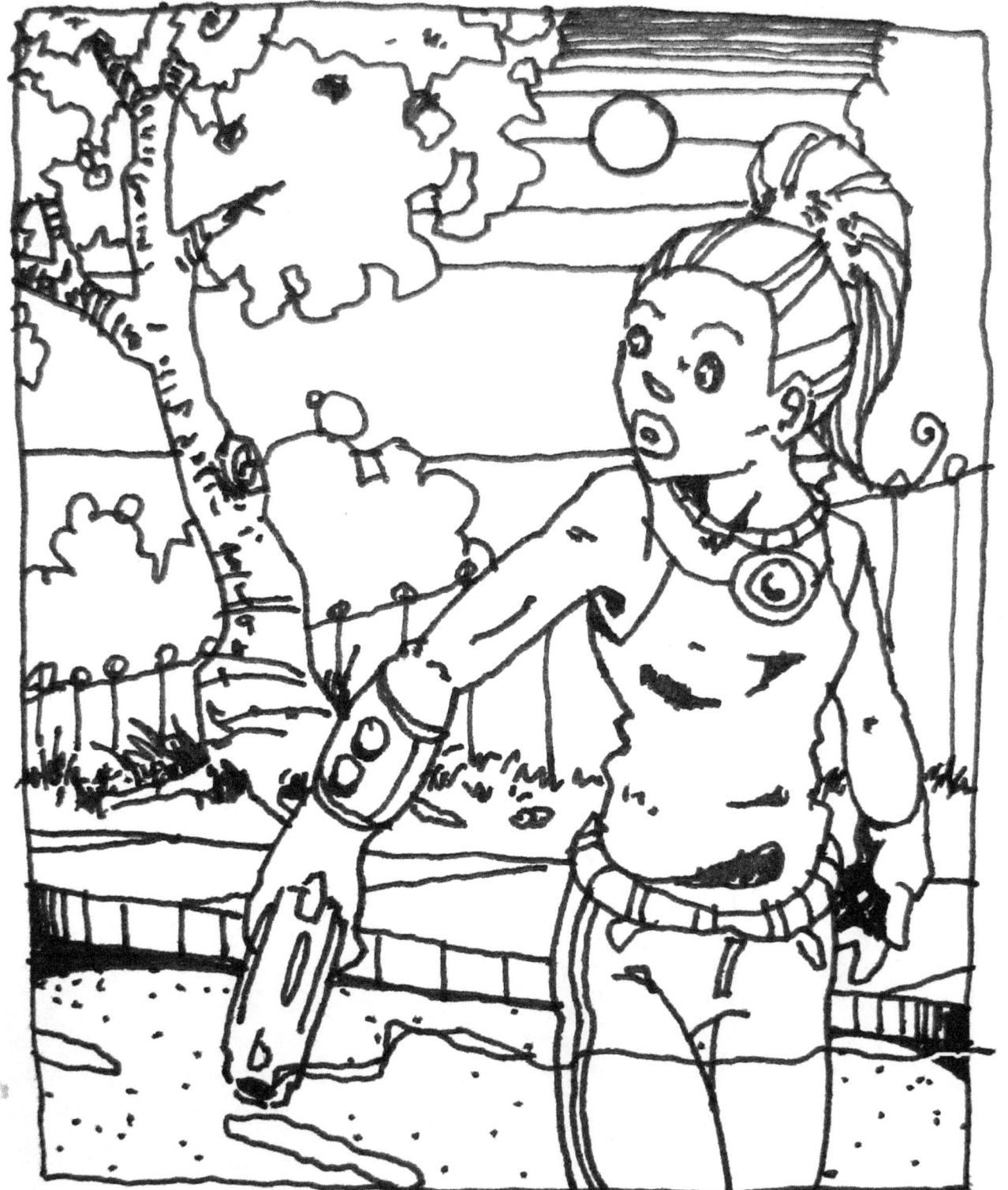

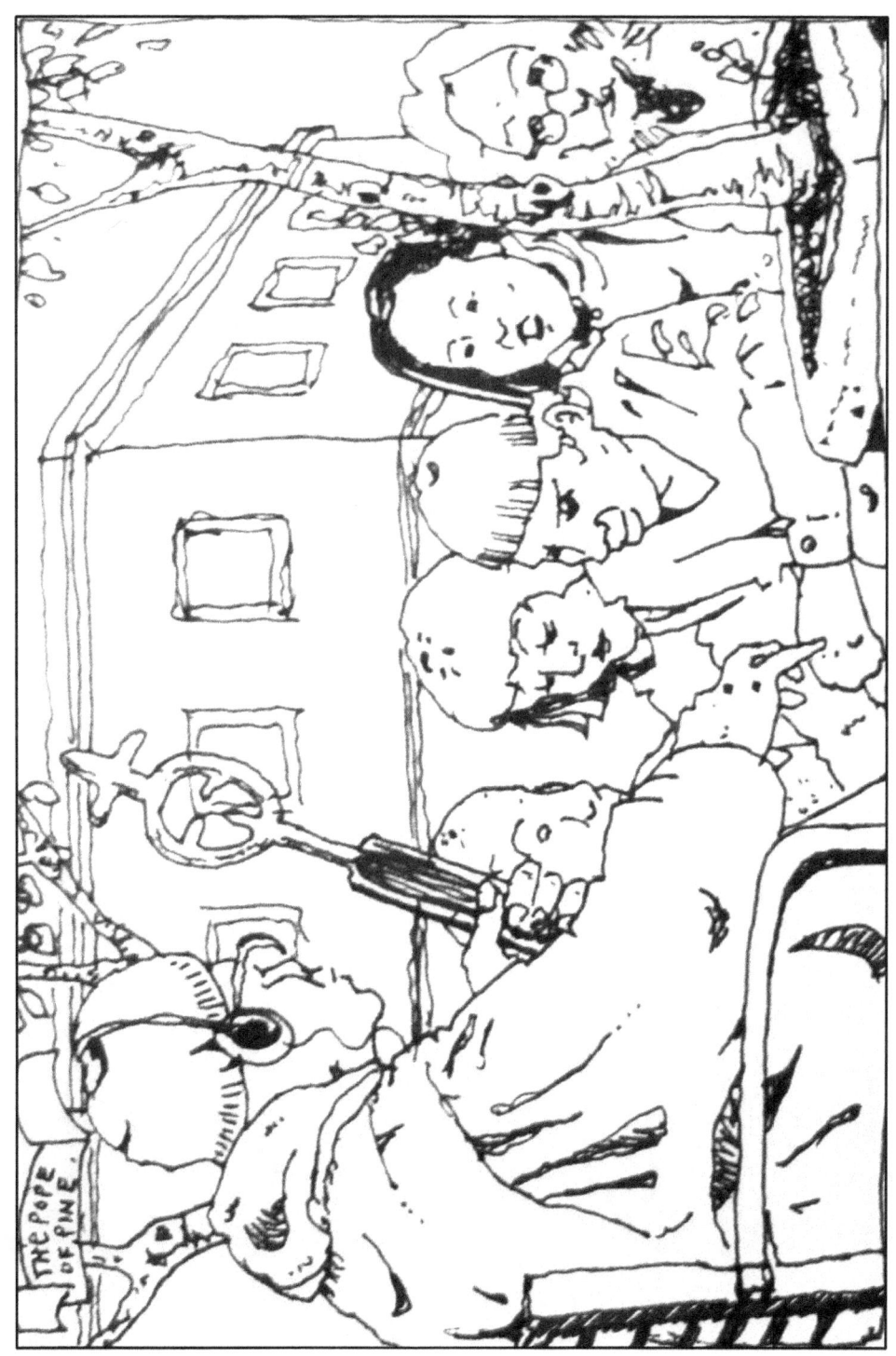

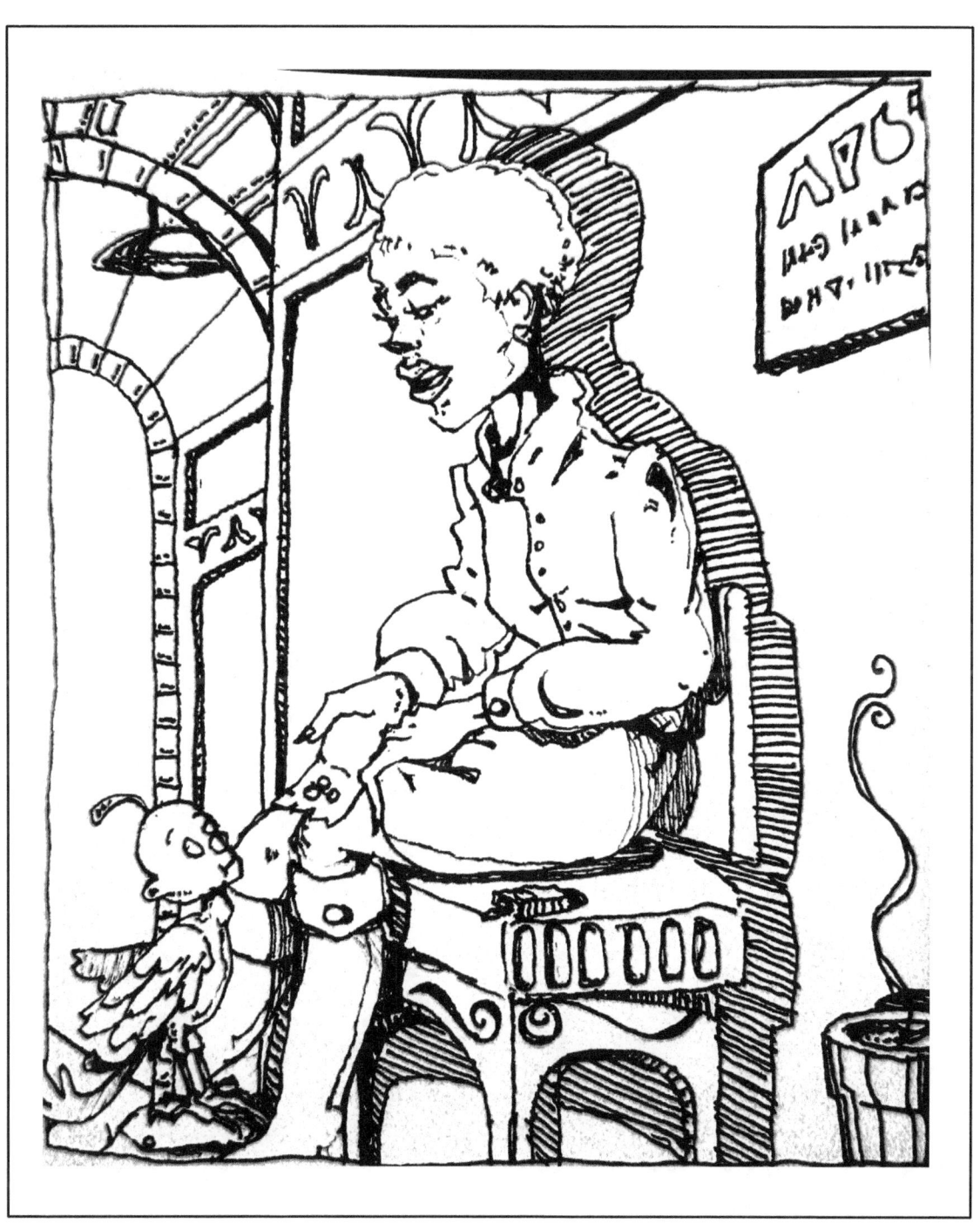

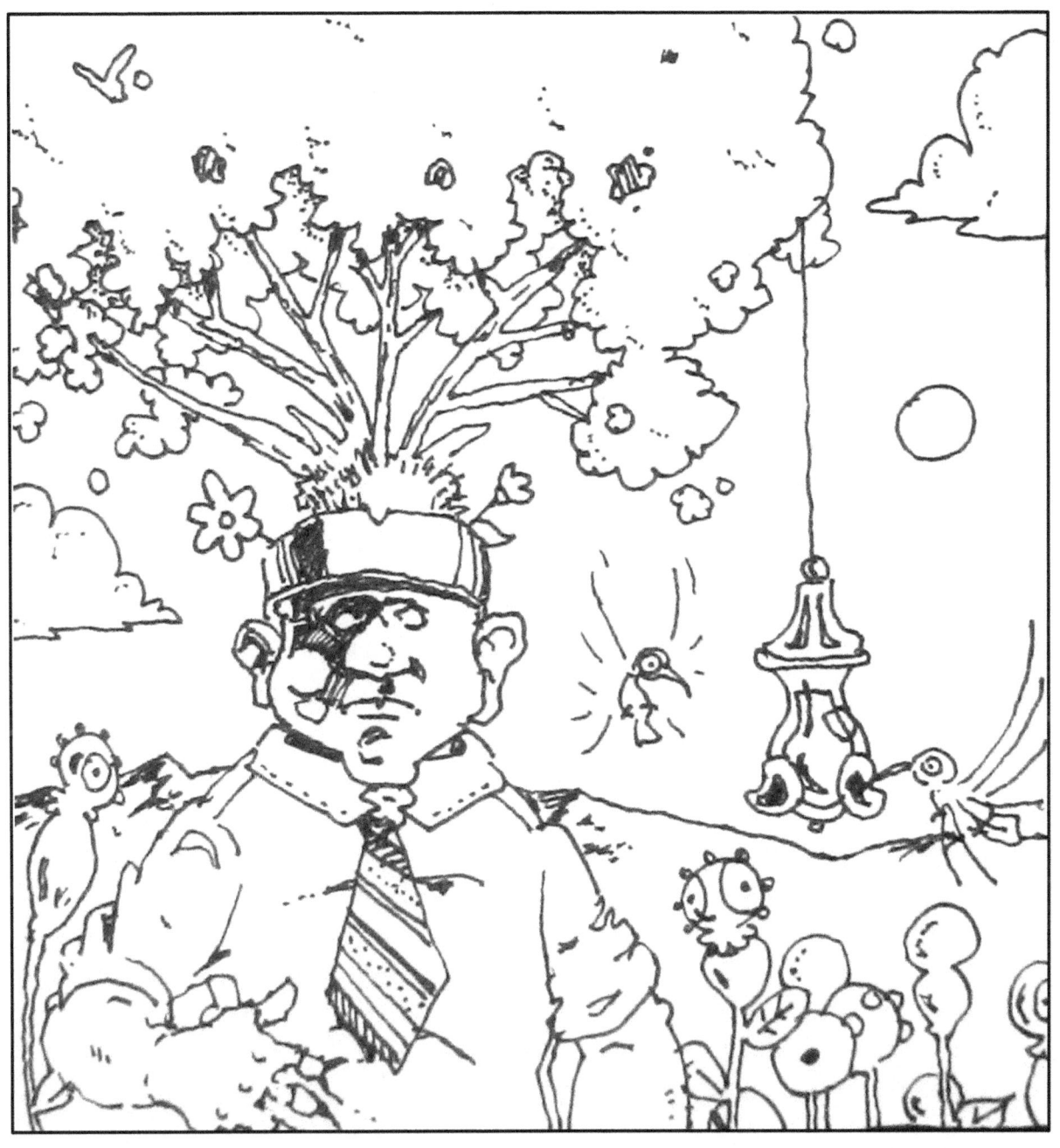

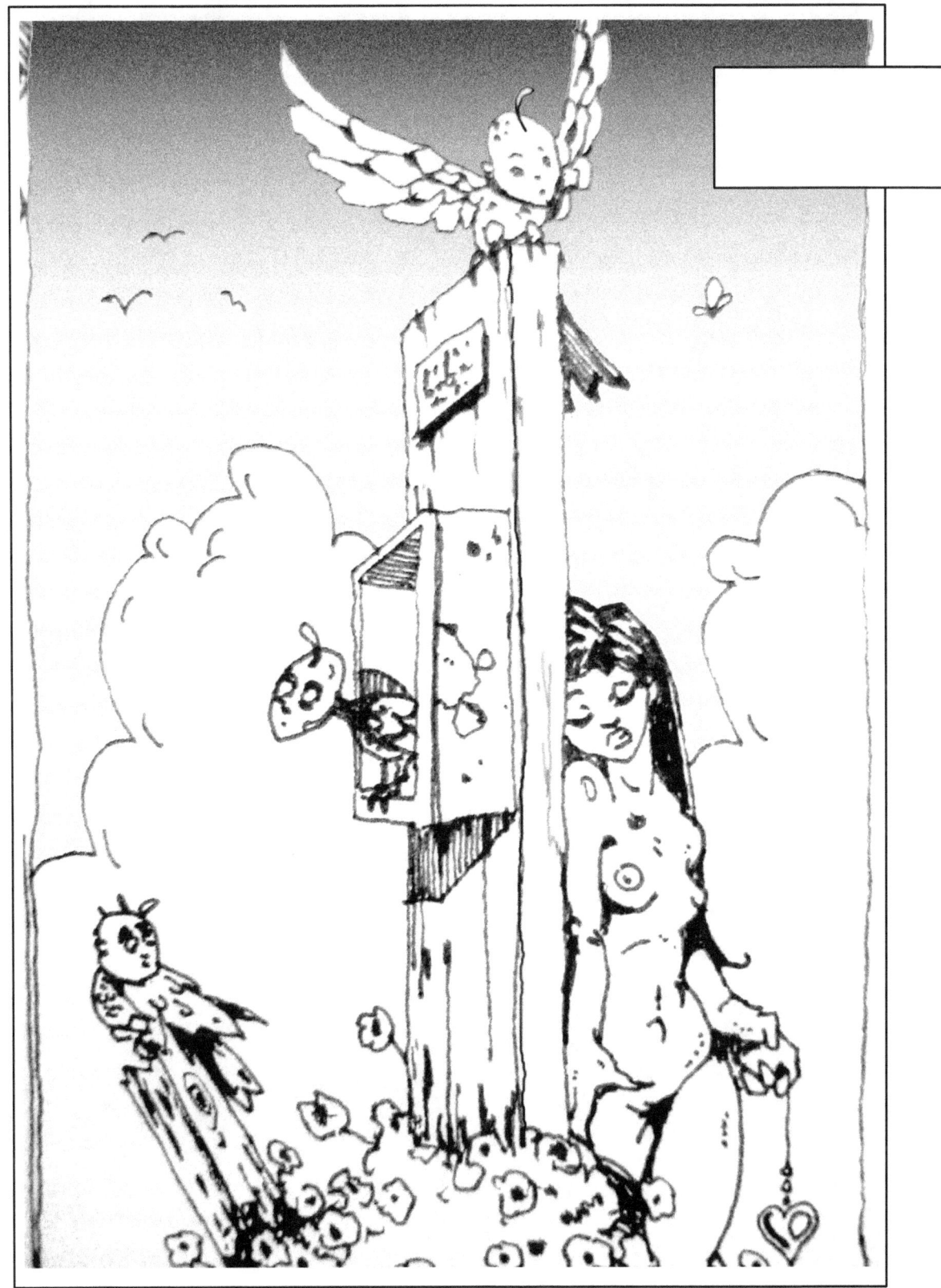

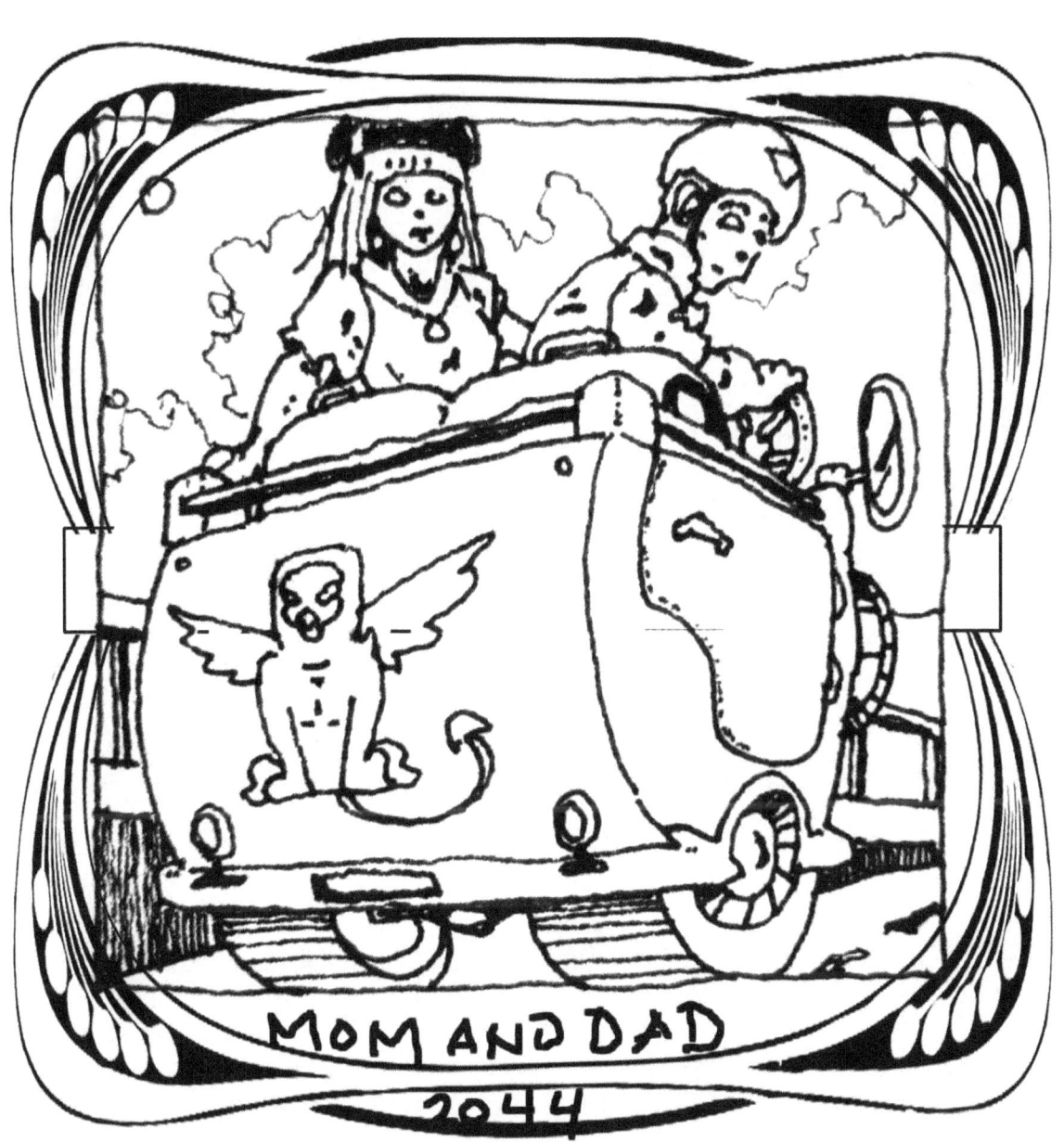

WHO NEEDS FOUR WHEELS?

www.ingramcontent.com/pod-product-compliance
Lightning Source LLC
Chambersburg PA
CBHW080645180526
45168CB00008B/3311